THE PHILOSOPHICAL AND THEOLOGICAL
FOUNDATIONS OF ETHICS

Also by Peter Byrne

ETHICS AND LAW IN HEALTH CARE AND RESEARCH (*editor*)
HEALTH, RIGHTS AND RESOURCES (*editor*)
MEDICINE IN CONTEMPORARY SOCIETY (*editor*)
MEDICINE, MEDICAL ETHICS AND THE VALUES OF LIFE (*editor*)
NATURAL RELIGION AND THE NATURE OF RELIGION
RELIGION DEFINED AND EXPLAINED (*with Peter Clarke*)
RIGHTS AND WRONGS IN MEDICINE (*editor*)

The Philosophical and Theological Foundations of Ethics

An Introduction to Moral Theory and its Relation to Religious Belief

PETER BYRNE

Lecturer in the Philosophy of Religion
King's College, London

St. Martin's Press

First published in Great Britain 1992 by
THE MACMILLAN PRESS LTD
Houndmills, Basingstoke, Hampshire RG21 2XS
and London
Companies and representatives
throughout the world

A catalogue record for this book is available
from the British Library.

ISBN 0–333–55494–9

Printed in Great Britain by
Antony Rowe Ltd
Chippenham, Wiltshire

11 10   9   8   7   6   5   4   3   2
03 02 01 00 99 98 97 96 95 94

First published in the United States of America 1992 by
Scholarly and Reference Division,
ST. MARTIN'S PRESS, INC.,
175 Fifth Avenue,
New York, N.Y. 10010

ISBN 0–312–07937–0

Library of Congress Cataloging-in-Publication Data
Byrne, Peter, 1950–
The philosophical and theoloigical foundations of ethics : an
introduction to moral theory and its relation to religious belief / Peter Byrne.
p. cm.
Includes bibliographical references and index.
ISBN 0–312–07937–0
1. Ethics.   2. Religion and ethics.   I. Title.
BJ1012.B97   1992
170—dc20   91–44846
                                                                CIP

Contents

Preface

This book is intended as an introductory survey of moral philosophy with a particular emphasis on the relationship between morality and religious belief. The aim is to explain and discuss some of the major issues in moral philosophy, tracing, as the account proceeds, their implications for an understanding of how religion might bear on ethics. The book is meant therefore to be of particular help to students of moral theology and religious studies who need an introduction to moral theory. One way in which such students meet moral philosophy nowadays is in the context of practical ethics. It has come to be assumed that in fields such as medical ethics it is essential to know moral philosophy and moral theory in order to discuss practical moral problems. Hence, we have the coinage 'philosophical medical ethics' – used to characterise critical thinking about the ethics of medical practice. I have written with one eye on the notion that moral philosophy is the foundational discipline in practical ethics. During the course of my argument I shall suggest that there are grave limitations in this idea, arising out of the nature of moral knowledge. But there are some lessons to be learnt from moral philosophy for practical ethics, and I have drawn them when appropriate.

Readers should be warned that this study is biased in certain directions. Its interest in morality's relation to religion inclines it to objectivism in ethics and to giving, from the start, an account of moral knowledge and moral experience which will make dialogue between secular and religious moral thinkers intelligible. Its lack of neutrality is I hope compensated by the fact that it offers an argument for a positive, distinctive view of the nature of moral thought, so that at least those who disagree with this view will see what has to be defended and attacked if it is to work at all. In the interests of getting on with an uncluttered argument and exposition I have kept references and textual notes to a minimum.

Before the rise of interest in practical ethics in philosophy departments it was common to find moral philosophy characterised as a purely formal, 'second-order' discipline. Some argue that it has no concern with the content of moral judgement but merely with the formal structure of moral argument and experience. It does not seek to know what is good but rather what the meaning of 'good' and related words might be. Such a characterisation of the subject is satisfactory only in so far as there is an intelligible distinction between form and content in morals. Moral philosophy has traditionally had other tasks, notably the discovery and examination of the most basic goods, virtues and moral principles. In the course of this 'first-order' task moral philosophers past and present perforce offer comment on the nature and distinguishing features of moral judgement but they go beyond comment on the 'form' of ethics. There is every reason to persevere with this second, older characterisation of the moral philosopher's task. It is truer to the history of the subject and reflects even contemporary practice better. Even the strictest formalists in modern moral philosophy have found it hard to refrain from drawing implications from their accounts of the meaning of moral judgement for the nature of the most basic goods, virtues and principles of right. There appears reason to expect that any account of the form of morality will set limits upon, or suggest requirements for, an acceptable content of morality.

The above registers the conviction that the distinction between form and content in morality is a hazy one at best. Students should be particularly wary, in my view, of the vision of the subject which ties it to description of the special features of 'the language of morals', as if moral philosophy's task were the tracking down of a special type of meaning and a special type of vocabulary peculiar to morals. While this might lead to a sharp distinction between second- and first-order reflections on morals, there is ground to question whether there is any special form of meaning attaching to words in moral contexts. Moreover, though there are terms characteristic of moral judgement (such as the words for the human virtues), many words used in moral discussion are equally at home outside it (see Wertheimer 1972 for well-argued doubts about whether there is a 'language of morals').

Morality as conceived in this book is a body of knowledge about how human beings ought to act. Moral philosophy has the task of setting out the structure of this body of knowledge and outlining its leading principles and ideas. Some might think that this begs straightaway the question of whether an objectivist or subjectivist account of moral thought is correct. The reasoning behind a subjectivist portrayal of morals will be discussed in Chapter 1. But we can see at once that any thinker who takes the possibility of a religious basis to ethics seriously has strong ground for assuming that such reasoning is fallacious and that only the view that morality is a branch genuine knowledge will do.

It cannot be denied that there are subjectivist accounts of morals which try to establish an intelligible link between religion and ethics (Braithwaite 1966 is a clear if simple example). Yet there will always be a substantial cost to embracing subjectivism in ethics from within a religious outlook. It will entail a corresponding subjectivism in doctrine and related problems in the conception of the sacred. It is one of humanity's key ideas about the sacred that it is worthy of devotion or worship and is in some manner the source of moral and other values. It is difficult to entertain the thought that value is some form of human invention or projection and not draw the consequence that divinity is likewise a humanly produced fiction. If I take away from my conception of divinity all that contains judgements of value, on the ground that such judgements are in no real sense objectively true or known to be true, then what is left will hardly be intelligible as a portrayal of the independently sacred. In consistency an account of the sacred as a human projection must follow, and while such accounts can indeed be found they are hard to reconcile with traditional belief or with the task of doctrinal reflection (compare Cupitt 1980). Whether or not morality is dependent on religion we shall discuss in Chapter 7 and 8, but it certainly appears as if religion is dependent on morality to the extent that if the idea of moral truth is an illusion, then so is that of religious truth.

1

The Nature and Objectivity of Morality

THE FORM OF MORALITY

One of the crucial tasks of moral philosophy appears to be that of defining morality. This might be one early way in which reflection on the form of morals suggests limits to its content. The customary understanding of what morality is might indeed rule out various modes of thought and action as options for ethics.

Though inviting, this method for quickly narrowing our sights in the search for the fundamentals of ethics is open to objection. It is evidently wrong to settle substantive questions on important topics by definitional fiat or appeal to ordinary usage. Somehow we must balance our proper search for an initial definition of morality with the need not to beg important questions. It is right to look to the definition of morality for hints in structuring enquiry into the nature of moral knowledge, while seeing any principles that definition yields as rebuttable and in need of independent justification should they prove controversial in later passages of argument. For example, I shall indicate below how a certain conception of morality's universality is implicit in its customary definition and how this conception entails *prima facie* problems for the view that moral knowledge depends on religious knowledge. This will not settle questions about the relationship of religion to morality by itself. But it will draw our attention to a range of human experience which counts against some accounts of that relationship.

By 'morality' we do not mean in this study customary, established thought about conduct and our enquiry into the relation between religion and morality does not concern the historical or sociological facts about the influence of religion on behaviour. It is assumed here that within the history of customary moral ideas we can find

1

a body of critical thought and experience (that is: knowledge) about what is good/bad and right/wrong for human beings. The task of characterising the nature of this critical thought about conduct through definition is that of picking out the key features of the typical judgements that are constitutive of critical morality. The features I select are endorsed in many studies of the definition of morality (see especially Green 1978:13–35). They are: practicality, rationality, universality, impartiality, and authority.

The practical character of morality stems from its membership of the broad genus of 'thought about human action'. The breadth of this genus is indicated by the fact that it includes all other systems of rules about conduct and other practical sciences. The major problem in the definition of morality concerns the distinguishing features of morality as a system of thought about human action. However, we must note at this early stage that morality is not simply directed to answering questions about how we are to act. We appraise people's feelings and perceptions from a moral point of view as well as their conduct. As we shall indicate in discussing the nature of action and of virtue, 'conduct' so far as ethics is concerned refers to a complex of motive and intention as well as outward action. With these qualifications understood we may continue to think of morality as a distinctive form of thought about conduct.

One of the distinguishing features of thought about conduct that is ethical is that it is based upon reasons. We expect moral judgements to approve/disapprove of acts on the basis of facts about them which constitute reasons for those judgements. A technical way of expressing this thought about moral judgements is through saying that the characteristics they impute to actions are 'supervenient'. The goodness or rightness of an act supervenes on those other properties it possesses which are the grounds for thinking it good or right. Compare expressions of taste: I eat ice cream and I like doing so, but neither my action nor my pleasure rests upon a reason. Moreover, we expect moral judgements to be commendable to others on the basis of reasons. It would always appear appropriate to ask for the reasons behind the acceptance of any candidate moral rule or principle as correct.

The universality of moral judgements is closely linked to their rationality. Universality is to be distinguished from generality. Moral judgements can vary from very general principles to more specific moral rules and down to detailed comments on what a given individual ought or ought not to do. (The distinction between rules and principles will be set out more clearly in Chapter 3). But even a detailed judgement, such as that 'Byrne should not steal ideas from his students' essays', has a universal force. It will be based upon a reason (for example: stealing ideas is cheating and cheating causes resentment) which will entail that a corresponding judgement will be applicable to anyone else where that same reason applies. Any judgement based on a ground is universal in its implications. It will always be a mark of irrationality to refuse to make a similar judgement about a similar case unless a relevant difference can be cited between them. Any reasoned judgement implicitly invokes a rule which then has universal force.

Some writers (notably Hare 1963:10–13) contend that this formal feature of moral judgements, entailed by their being members of the class of judgements based on reasons, entails that no moral rules can be expressed in terms which make essential reference to particular persons. This is then an alternative account of the universalisability of moral judgements: they cannot rest on reasons/rules which make essential reference to particular people (or times or places). Now it is true that we expect moral judgements from their very nature to be based on reasons which have a certain impartiality. Someone who reasons about what to do and not to do solely by reference to reasons relating to what will further his or her private interests is hardly thinking morally. But this impartiality is not a simple consequence of the universalisability that comes from a judgement based upon reasons. It must rather be based on more substantive considerations about the nature of morality.

Let us suspend disbelief so far as to imagine that my judgements about conduct are based consistently on the principle that the well-being of Peter Byrne is the highest good in the universe. Note that I can reason in a universal and consistent way that if this good makes something right for me it makes a corresponding action right for anyone else in similar circumstances. In other words: other people should reason how to act in the light of the requirement to maximise Byrne's well-being. My principles of conduct are utterly egoistical in content, yet perfectly universalisable in their form. So it appears mistaken to argue that the universal force attaching to moral judgements which arises out of their being based upon reasons entails any restriction on the content of moral principles, such as that they should not make reference to particular persons (see Munro 1967:204–7 for a full defence of this point).

The above comments about the universal force of moral judgements will prove important in the discussion of some contemporary moral theories, but they indicate immediately that something more is needed to justify our presumption that morality should embody some form of impartial stance upon conduct. What is required is a further aspect of morality's universality, namely the idea that any moral judgement, rule or principle be something that could be openly recommended to all as something that they could agree with and follow. Here we have the idea that moral judgements are by definition the opposite of the code of a sect or private group. Any requirement on conduct which I could not imagine commending to all is not a moral requirement. What I can commend for others' agreement and acceptance is what I think all can see there is good reason to accept as rational requirement on action. It is this which makes Byrnean egoism a dubious bases for a morality: only the most fantastic set of beliefs about my place in the universe could give me ground to suppose that all rational people could come to see Byrne's good as the ultimate good. Only principles which embody some kind of distance from my own private desires and some concern with the good of all stand a chance of universal acceptance.

It is this requirement in the definition of morality that creates a problem at the start of any investigation of the relationship between morality and religion. Given this requirement, it appears to be impossible to allow that knowledge or possession of any given religious faith is a precondition of moral knowledge. For if it were, then only those with that faith could be expected to accept and endorse moral principles. Moral principles could not be commendable to all. The precise and further implications of this idea will be explored in later chapters. For the moment let us note that it appears to entail that every human being can be expected to have what it takes rationally to consider and accept moral judgement just in virtue of being a (at least: rational and adult) human being. Restricted or secret forms of knowledge and awareness are excluded if morality's universality can be defended.

As indicated above the settling of debatable questions by definition is to be avoided. Surely, someone might argue, it is possible to conceive that the good sought in morality was only graspable by those who had a religious belief of some sort, entailing that this good was not cognisable by those outside the faith. However, we must remind ourselves what lies behind the universality requirement as I have described it. We should all feel unease at moral judgements offered on grounds which could not be communicated to all. We are inclined to regard the codes of such esoteric groups as Freemasons as having moral import only to the extent that their ideas can be translated and defended in a common currency of moral thought. Above all, we take it that if someone has done moral wrong he or she can be blamed provided that he or she has a normal grasp of the circumstances and is of normal intelligence. Moral requirements cannot bind all and be the standard of correctness for all if only some can be aware of them. This does not rule out religious faith making a contribution to knowledge of the good aimed at in morality, but its contribution must be capable of appreciation and acceptance by the general run of moral agents. The exact nature of this requirement needs to be explored below (in Chapter 8 in particular). *Prima facie* it does rule out some of the more extreme claims that ethics is unintelligible without faith.

The impartiality that the extension of universality entails remains to be properly characterised. All would agree that it excludes from the statement of important moral principles notions that contain essential reference to particular persons (for the reasons given above). It thus allows a distinction between morality and the egoistic pursuit of self interest. Some writers (to be discussed in Chapter 5) consider that it entails that the basic principles of right can make no reference to any substantive picture of the human good or of the ideal way of life for human beings. Their ground is roughly that all such conceptions of the best way of life involve showing partiality to some favoured ways of life above others. Morality is then largely concerned with procedural principles for avoiding conflict and promoting equity between the pursuit of different preferred ways of life. We cannot debate this strict interpretation of the impartiality behind the moral point of view now. Another conception of that point of view, which appears to embody the stance of anti-egoism just as well can be outlined as follows.

What is characteristic of me when I make judgements from the moral point of view is that I reflect on what is proper and improper for me to do from the standpoint of what I consider proper and improper for a *human being* to do. If 'I shouldn't steal' is a moral judgement it is so because it embodies a thought about what human beings should not do. This why moral judgements are universalisable in the sense that I expect a valid judgement of mine to be capable of being commended to all reasonable people. When I am deciding how to act from the moral point of view I am deciding what is proper, fit, choiceworthy for a human being to do in the relevant circumstances. We think in universal terms when we think morally because we are considering what actions would constitute a fitting, noble, excellent way for a human being to live. It is but short step to conclude that a moral judgement embodies a conception of the human good. A conception of the human good is a picture of the proper, fitting, most praiseworthy way of life for a person to display. This would be another way of interpreting the notion of impartiality behind the moral point of view. Moral judgements are impartial, on this understanding, not in being abstracted from all conceptions of ends and ideals, but in being reflections of pictures of the ideal way of life for any human being to live. This is how I move up from the thought of what might be a good choice or action for me to what would be a good choice or action for anyone in my circumstances. Much more needs to be said by way of making this notion of a human good clearer and by way of distinguishing the two interpretations of impartiality offered here. This will be attempted in Chapters 4 to 6.

One further characteristic needs to mentioned in defining the nature of morality: authority. It would be odd to affirm that something was morally wrong but nonetheless that I ought to do it. Implicit in the ordinary use of moral judgements is the thought that they are overriding. It is moral judgements that, by definition, provide answers to questions about what is ultimately to be done or chosen. It is in this respect that morality has authority. It provides the final court of appeal in human conduct.

This feature of the nature of morality arouses suspicion in a number of philosophers. Conjoined with the other characteristics of morality mentioned here it entails that morality is a system of critical thought about conduct whose judgements are rational, universal, impartial and authoritative. But now this appears to make true by definition the proposition that the ultimate touchstones by which people reason about how to act have to be principles of universal, impartial right. But if this is true, it cannot be so by mere definition. For it is surely possible to imagine, if not discover, people whose ultimate touchstones of choice in conduct are opposed to or different from what ordinarily we would call moral judgements. (Villains in fact or fiction – such as Fielding's Jonathan Wild – are good examples of such folk.) If we wish to define moral judgements as those which are overriding, then we have to accept that this formal feature of morality entails nothing about its content. We might speak of a person's morality – meaning that set of judgements or principles which is overriding for him or her – but no limits are thereby set as to what principles an individual may think are of overriding importance. It is a contingent fact that most of us take judgements with a typical content to be overriding.

It has to be admitted that it is a substantial, not a mere definitional, truth that principles with the content of ordinary morality (for example, which appeal to respect for other's interests, which outlaw gratuitous harm and forbid the naked pursuit of self-interest) provide the final arbiters of correctness in conduct. However, we should not give up the important point that within our understanding of morality lies the belief that principles with a certain, loosely-defined content have a special authority and provide the final court of appeal in conduct. This belief is internally related to the other features central to our concept of morality. In particular the thought that morality is rational and universal in its claims suggests limits on its content. For if I think that a given act is morally right I think that the standard it embodies could be openly and rationally commended to all and it is hard to see how that can fail to point in the direction of a certain range of content for moral judgements. We have seen that it constrains us to show how our judgements embody a form of impartiality.

Two important concessions must be made to the formalist objection to the customary definition of morality. First it must be admitted that there can be different ways of interpreting the impartiality demanded of moral considerations. Differences in broad philosophical interpretations of this notion have already been pointed to. Even from within one such philosophical interpretation, for example that which connects impartiality with the idea of the human good, allowance can be made for vast differences over how to give substantive shape to that idea. While we might agree that morality has typically to do with respect for others, avoiding harm and the like, this is because we share a range of beliefs about where to find the best way of life for human beings. Others with different beliefs might offer quite different accounts of what considerations were morally important. The mind boggles at the thought of what I must believe about my own status in the universe to hold that the human good consists in all acting so as promote the happiness of Peter Byrne, but we can imagine how someone under the influence of a little bad philosophy could be convinced that the human good was to be achieved by each ruthlessly promoting his or her own interests to the exclusion of concern for others. Such a person would have an inverse picture to the customary one about what counted as morally commanded, but granted its background in an eccentric set of beliefs about human life and happiness, it would be a picture that fitted into the definition of morality offered here. A second concession to the formalist objection is the admission that it is a substantive (and therefore not unquestionable) proposition that a person's overriding principles of action should reflect conceptions of what is fitting and proper for human beings to choose and of what can be commended to others. Perhaps there are or can be people who reach decisions about what is ultimately important in conduct while rejecting any concern with what is impartially right or choiceworthy for human beings as such.

If this latter concession is correctly made, then the belief that ultimate and overriding principles of conduct must make reference to considerations of an impartial kind stands in need of justification. The definition of morality in that event embodies a point of view about the centrality of certain kinds of considerations in human life which requires independent defence and articulation. It may be that, for all that morality provides a point of view upon conduct that claims to be rational, universal, impartial and authoritative, it is nonetheless an illusory point of view. Maybe no point of view on action that is universal and impartial can be rationally commended or defended as authoritative. This introduces the topic of moral scepticism.

THE OBJECTIVITY OF MORALITY

The type of thought and experience we call 'moral' claims on the surface to be a form of knowledge. We recognise in moral discourse statements which are mere expressions of opinion and prejudice, questions which have no real answers because they are badly posed, and conclusions which have no ground in genuine reasons. But such common defects in moral thought are seen in the light of contrasts with yet other moral statements which have the status of reasoned opinions and truths. We make contrasts within morality between that which has a genuine claim to objectivity and that which is merely the expression of personal, unreasoned prejudice. Making this contrast, we assume that the progress of moral thought is one that involves the escape from a partial, personal, preference-based view toward genuinely inter-subjective claims tested by reflection. We would have no hesitation in ordinary speech in saying that it was true that racial discrimination is unjust. We naturally carry over the cognitive vocabulary of discovery, truth and reason from reflection about matters scientific, historical and the like into thought about how we should act as human beings (see White 1970:57–65).

Now all this could be an illusion. It may be that there is nothing worthy of the name of knowledge to be had of universal, authoritative principles of conduct. It may be that our use of the vocabulary and structures of cognitive enquiry is a mere mask which hides the fact that moral judgements are nothing other than the expression of personal preference or socially-imposed rules. As indicated above, there is strong reason from within a theological perspective to assume that scepticism of this type is ungrounded, for if moral thought falls to scepticism, religious thought will follow. (But note: some might argue that only by assuming a religious basis to ethics can moral scepticism be properly dealt with – see Chapter 7.) I shall assume therefore that scepticism about moral knowledge is to be resisted. The strategy for opposing it is inevitably complex and includes the following elements: (i) Treating it as being just as controversial as scepticism about other elements of our common sense view of the world; (ii) Setting it the target of showing that there are factors which destroy the cognitivity of morals which would not at the same time destroy the cognitivity of other branches of human enquiry; (iii) Showing the limitations of the main arguments advanced in favour of it.

Defending the cognitivity of moral thought should not be taken to involve offering a particular metaphysical account of what moral terms refer to or what reality moral truths describe. Here, as in other areas of philosophy, we rapidly get into deep and murky waters if we try to say just what truth and correspondence to reality consist in. It matters more that we can be clear about the consequences of employing the notion of truth and its relatives in association with an area of discourse. These include the ideas that disagreements in this area can be explained through failures in, or disruptions to, the operations of deliberation, reason, argument and the like. By contrast, agreement in opinion is, sometimes at least, to be explained by all that it is entailed in saying that different enquirers have come to a shared discovery of the truth. Cognitivity involves the presumption that the evolution of opinion in the area in question will show a convergence on truth and an accumulation of truths (compare Wiggins 1991). This entails that the cognitivity of morals can only be finally defended in the light of a convincing account of how reason and discovery operates in moral thought. But prior to that account some provisional discussion of the case for and against scepticism can be offered.

Moral scepticism can be introduced by reference to two arguments for it: that from relativity and disagreement and that from the 'queerness' of moral properties.

Some contend that the extent of disagreement on what is right and good for human beings between and within human cultures shows that moral thought is the inevitable outcome and expression of cultural conditioning and tradition. Within a culture, or tradition that contributes to a culture, we can conceive of there being argument directed toward achieving agreement, but between cultures and traditions only irresolvable conflicts are to be expected.

The problem with this as an argument for moral scepticism is that it is in danger of proving too much or too little. If we stress the great extent of divergence between social and intellectual traditions (or whole cultures), we can hardly fail to notice that this divergence takes in opinions on matters other than morals: on human nature, cosmology and history, for example. Indeed, the moral divergence between cultural traditions can be argued to grow out of and be enmeshed in disagreements in these other areas. The defender of cognitivism in morals can claim that is not as if moral disagreement arises *despite* unanimity on larger views of human nature, the cosmos and the meaning of history. It is the embeddedness of opinions about the good and the right in such larger conceptions that appears to create the problem the relativist picks upon. If moral thought is relative in some important way to cultures or cultural traditions, it might be because other, non-moral opinions are. Further, it is hard to see why noting such disagreements should not simply be a way of drawing attention to the form any intellectual attempts to reach agreement in morals will have to take: they will have to begin by tackling the cultural assumptions that create divergence. It may be argued that such attempts are doomed to failure. Why? If they are doomed because of the total incommensurability of moral systems across traditions, it will be because of the incommensurablity of the ways of looking at humanity and the world in which these systems are embedded. So the relativity of much more than morals will follow. The problem remains of how we can have moral scepticism without general scepticism.

If we press the facts of moral disagreement too far they will swallow up other modes of discourse. On the other hand, we might be impressed by the extent to which moral agreement is possible across cultural traditions. Consider the extent to which many folk from different cultural and religious backgrounds have come to accept that capital punishment is wrong or that religious toleration is a good.

Cognitivism can rightly refuse to see the apparent diversity and relativity of morals as a decisive objection to its picture of the nature of moral thought to the extent that it can offer its own explanation of these facts. Some diversity and relativity can be accounted for on the simple hypothesis of human error intervening between the moral truth and its perception and some by reference to the embeddedness of moral conceptions in world views as described above. Yet other aspects of relativity can be explained through appealing to the contextual character of moral principles and moral thought. Unless the cognitivist has a liking for absolutism, he or she can believe that moral judgements sometime successfully discover truth while also admitting that what this truth consists in varies according to circumstance. We hope that engineers build bridges according to true principles of civil engineering and true calculations of the strengths of the particular structures they make. But how exactly a bridge is built is rightly varied according to the special circumstances of geology, load and materials of particular bridges. As a practical science, civil engineering applies right general notions in the light of specific facts to give unique answers to what is to be done in particular cases. Ethics is just such another practical science and it can quite properly claim to search for truth while disclaiming any interest in making the specifics of the right and the good the same for all, regardless of time, place and circumstance. It is actually a mark of the search for the truth in the rights and wrongs of human conduct, as in the search for the truth about how to build bridges, that the enquirer expects diversity in prescription and seeks out those factors that make true answers specific to particular circumstances. (More will be said about the role of circumstances in deciding rights and wrongs in Chapters 3 and 4).

Despite the fact that cognitivism obviously has internal resources for responding to relativity and disagreement in morals, the moral sceptic will not be content with the replies offered so far. He or she will contend that there is something special about the nature of moral disagreement which defeats the efforts of the cognitivist.

What this might be becomes clear when we move to further arguments for scepticism. The 'argument from queerness' was so labelled by the late JL Mackie (Mackie 1977:38–42). Its logic can be illustrated by the sample judgement 'Abortion is wrong'. Cognitivism appears to hold that such a judgement involves the perception (if true) of a quality in the acts mentioned which exists independent of human perception of them. (Contrast the bitterness in neat Scotch which some taste in it but true lovers of whisky do not. The bitterness, it might be said, is not in the Scotch but is a projection of a human reaction to it.) But how can this 'wrongness' be in the act when two people might agree about all the relevant observable facts about an act of abortion but one judge it right and another wrong? Nor is this 'wrongness' a fact about the act which can be deductively or inductively inferred from its perceived qualities. For disagreement about its alleged presence can survive not only agreement on its perceived qualities but also agreement on relevant principles of deduction and induction and on observable facts about other acts of abortion. Hence the 'queerness' of moral qualities. There seems no clear sense in which they are observable, nor is their presence inferrable, deductively or inductively, from any observable facts. Is it not then obvious that moral terms do not denote qualities in acts at all?

The argument from queerness leads to the conclusion that moral qualities are not in reality at all, but are projected onto the world of fact by human beings. Two people who differ over the wrongness of abortion do not disagree over any matter of fact but over the reactions they offer to the common facts they are both aware of. They differ in the attitudes, preferences or desires they bring to bear on those facts. The 'wrongness' or 'rightness' they see in the facts is nothing other than a projection of the attitudinal states in themselves that the facts give rise to. Out of the argument from queerness grows the idea of a distinction between facts and values. Facts are in reality. Values are not, rather they are projected onto it by human beings with their preferences, desires and the like. Moral judgements turn out to be misleading as to their true form. They may be phrased in the indicative mood. We may use the language of truth and falsity of them, but they do not in reality express propositions which have a truth value. They express preferences and desires, or are analogous to imperatives, differing from simple commands mainly in their universal form. If value exists only as projected preference, then we should expect to find that moral disagreements cannot be resolved by appeal to the facts surrounding any issue. One who believes in the opposition between matters of fact and value that arises out of the thought that values are projected preferences will expect that the central, typical case of moral disagreement will be one where the parties are agreed an all matters – factual, logical, inductive – relevant to the issue in dispute and where disagreement is simply the clash of different sets of attitudes applied to the same beliefs about what is the case. For such a thinker the embedded character of moral disagreements noted above is an inconvenient disguise of the true nature of moral dispute.

The fact value distinction has a simple explanation of a key feature of moral judgements implicit in our earlier account of their character: their action-guiding force. One who accepted that 'Cheating is wrong' would normally thereby be taken to have expressed a commitment about how he or she was to act in future. The practical force of moral judgements is linked to their assumed authority and to the fact that they provide, or register the presence of, reasons for action. The projectionist view of value fits in with a simple view of the nature of reasons for action which has dominated much recent philosophical writing on the subject (for a full treatment see McNaughton 1988:21–3 and *passim*). On this account actions are generated by a combination of an agent's beliefs and desires. An agent's desires give him or her certain goals to pursue; his or her beliefs provide awareness of occasions for acting so as to realise those goals. A combination of appropriate belief and desire sufficiently explains any minimally rational action. Moral judgement fits easily into this simple picture: it registers the existence of distinctive desires or preferences which when united with information about matters of fact yield reasons for action. If we accept that desire and belief are sharply distinguished, heterogeneous mental contents then all the following appear to hold. Any moral judgement can always be divided into an element expressive of beliefs about matters of fact and element of desire. The belief element cannot dictate the direction of the desire element. No belief about a matter of fact in isolation from a desire can provide a reason for action. No consistent scheme of moral judgement can ever be proved wrong or unreasonable by reference to the facts. Irresolvable moral disagreement despite complete factual agreement is always possible. Moral beliefs on this view motivate simply because they are not strictly beliefs:

they register a non-cognitive attitude of desire or aversion to acts and states of affairs. So the will has been committed in agreeing to a moral judgement.

The projectionist account of moral values and the allied fact value distinction present a powerful and many-faceted case for a subjectivist, non-cognitivist account of morals. I do not attempt to refute it fully here, but merely to indicate *prima facie* problems in it, the existence of which will justify us in pressing forward with an account of how morality might exist as a form of knowledge and how belief in God might influence that account. (A full discussion and, in my view refutation, of projectionism can be found in McNaughton 1988.)

One point we must insist on is that the fact value distinction is a form of moral scepticism, as such it is counter to our experience of morality and runs foul of our readiness to associate moral judgement with the language of truth and reason. Upholders of the distinction endeavour to escape this difficulty by insisting that there are restraints on acceptable moral schemes even within a projectionist account of value. They do so by stressing the strenuous nature of the requirement that a minimally rational moral scheme must be consistent. In the hands of R. M. Hare consistency gets elevated into a version of universalisability which entails real alleged limits on the substance of the moral schemes that human preferences can project onto the world, so much that in Hare's *Moral Thinking* we are told that consistency-as-universalisability limits the rational moral thinker solely to a version of utilitarianism as the only live option for a scheme of valuation to bring to bear on the facts (an argument to be fully discussed in Chapter 4). I regard this as fundamentally mistaken, for the reasons drawn from Munro (1967) above: Hare confuses the limited demands made by consistency on possible schemes of valuation with the substantive demands of impartiality. Other writers, while insisting that morality is 'invented' have pointed to the practical limits (provided, for example, by human sociability) on the moral schemes that human desire will dictate.

All such attempts to mitigate the moral scepticism implicit in the fact value distinction will nonetheless fail to capture the thought that judgements of moral worth are called forth by the facts of the circumstances in which we act. All will posit a strong element of illusion in moral experience. For when I 'perceive' that an action is wrong, I am, on the projectionist view of value, merely reading off the result produced by the projection my own preferences onto the world. I am tracing a feature of my own consciousness rather than of reality itself. When I say that I *know* that murder is wrong, or that human beings ought not to be enslaved, I would not in strictness be correct. Yet it seems natural to assume that if I know anything at all, I know these things. This is *prima facie* reason to see the projectionist theory of moral value as being counter-intuitive to same degree as other forms of scepticism (compare Bambrough 1979:14ff).

The argument from queerness insinuates that the experience of perceiving the moral worth of an action or agent must be illusory because moral qualities are too unlike ordinary perceptual properties, nor yet can their presence be inferred from perceptual qualities. This is a line of reasoning fed by a one-sided diet of examples. Many facts and qualities we perceive in the world are physical ones which we would expect to open to the view of anyone with normal sensory apparatus. But to suppose that physical properties are the only ones available to human judgement is to ignore the range of levels of meaning in the world around us. As well as seeing the shape of someone's face, I can see the anguish in it. I can hear the delight in a voice as well as its loudness. I can note the ethereal quality of a Turner landscape as well as the disposition of the colours on the canvass. Along with the physical shape of the words of a printed poem, I can discern the irony in them.

This last example clearly illustrates the point that meaning and significance may be there before us in the objects we attend to, even though it may be hidden to those who have all their senses in working order. Someone with a limited grasp of poetic convention or a too-literal mind might be able to understand the individual words in the poem but still fail to see its irony. What he or she lacks is the ability to detect a level of significance in what is before the eyes and the ability to see a relationship between these words and other similar examples of irony. Seeing the irony is not an inference which the unskilled could be led to make if only they were given the right inductive or deductive principles to apply to these words. It is rather the result of the exercise of judgement and discernment. This judgement and discernment can be passed on and there can be rational arguments about its correct exercise. Two critics might agree on the text of the poem but still disagree about whether it had an ironic meaning. Their disagreement could persist even though they were in agreement on what words were before them and on all relevant principles of inductive and deductive inference. What they would disagree about is the way in which this example of poetic speech stood in relation to others. Each would place it in a different range of examples. Argument between them might proceed by each trying to persuade the other that it to be seen along with these cases but as different from yet others. Here there is room for the exercise of reason even though the physical facts are established and no question of disputed inductive or deductive inferences from those facts is relevant (see Byrne 1979:270–1). It would be natural to say that if one of the parties vindicated his initial judgement about the meaning of the poem through the careful presentation of parallel cases, that he or she had shown the initial *perception* of the presence or absence of irony was correct.

It would be decidedly odd to say that because the anguish in the face, the delight in the voice, the irony in the words were not physical realities or deducible from physical realities by any strict procedure, they were therefore projected onto physical reality by the mind. Though non-physical, such realities are objective in so far as they are the object of judgements which can be true or false. And 'true' in these cases has the same formal properties as in the case of judgements about physical reality. For example, we should expect truths to be justifiable to and shareable with others; we should expect all true judgements to be consistent with one another; we should expect reasoning about such matters to lead to convergence in opinion. The argument from queerness trades on the thought that only physical reality is perceptible, only scientifically discoverable properties exist independently of human consciousness. The defender of the objectivity of moral value can rightly object that a whole series of levels of meaning in our experience would be condemned on this view to subjectivity. The range of perceptible, shareable, inter-subjectively testable reality extends beyond the physical.

The defender of the fact value distinction can still argue his or her case for the queerness of moral values if it can be shown that the practical force of moral judgements is such that they must be expressions of desire or preference rather than recognitions of qualities that exist independently of human agents. This practical force undoubtedly exists. Recognising that an act is morally appropriate/inappropriate is normally taken to involve in itself committing oneself to act as circumstances arise. Indeed, moral judgements involve recognition of overriding commitments to action. Somehow pointing to an agent's perception of an act's moral rightness explains in itself why he chose to do it.

The projectionist's account of these facts is based on some very general views about the nature and explanation of action. The key to them is the thought that beliefs cannot move actions on their own. Desires move actions. So my perception that it is right to be kind to my students cannot explain why I am moved to be kind if this 'perception' is productive of a mere *belief* that acts of kindness have a certain property (rightness). If my judgement about kindness being right is explanatory of my conduct it must be a roundabout way of expressing a preference and not the result of a perception yielding a belief. It can't be a cognitive state but must be a desiring state. A moral judgement expresses beliefs about the non-moral qualities of a case plus a preference about how to respond to such qualities. This is how a person's moral judgements can explain his or her actions.

Since this objection to objectivism in ethics is based on highly abstract and ramified issues in the philosophy of mind and action, it cannot be fully discussed here. It is enough for our purposes if we set out the main issues involved and the kinds of response that an objectivist account of moral value can offer.

Behind the objection is what is termed 'the belief-desire' theory or reasons for action, that is the theory that a combination of desires and beliefs can explain or justify conduct (McNaughton 1988:106ff). Taken in one way this theory is innocuous, if not truistic. My perception that an action is thoughtful, kind, considerate only explains why I do it given that it gives rise to intentions, plans and purposes of mine. If we use 'desire' as an umbrella term for intentions, purposes and the like, the belief-desire theory of motivation is thus far correct. What remains to be proved is that desires (understood in this very general sense) are non-cognitive states which must be brought to bear on natural, physical facts to make those facts morally relevant – thus projecting moral value onto the world in the process. If desires can sometimes be cognitive states, and if moral judgements can therefore be both expressions of desire and recognitions of objective qualities in acts and agents, then the belief-desire theory may yet be true while leaving the cognitive character of morality unscathed.

To make the above response intelligible we need a distinction between two kinds of desires. Consider my desire for the taste of ice-cream. This is termed an unmotivated or sense-desire in the literature (Nagel 1978:29). I do not have the desire because I perceive properties in ice-cream which I think it appropriate to pursue. It is an immediate sense-reaction to a stimulus the ice-cream provides.

The desire is not a cognitive state in me. Having the desire explains why I eat ice-cream when offered it to the extent that we understand any sentient creature's reactions of pursuit or avoidance to sensory stimuli deemed to be pleasant or unpleasant. But my desire to be honest with students and colleagues is a rational or motivated desire. My judgement that the truth must be told is a cognitive state which explains how I come to desire to speak honestly. The desire is unintelligible in isolation from the perception of what is required of me that gives rise to it.

The projectionist theory of value requires that we have pre-given desires of a particular sort that may be called moral, which then give rise to commitments to action once confronted with appropriate circumstances for fulfilling them. Moral principles then sum up the character of these peculiarly moral preferences: they specify the natural or physical facts about which we have positive or negative moral preferences (so: 'Helping others is good', 'Breaking promises is wrong'). What makes two sets of circumstances morally alike is that they share the same, relevant natural qualities and that a consistent set of moral preferences are applied to them (for there are no moral qualities in the world to make cases alike and circumstances only have moral relevance if they connect with a pre-given preference in the agent). The defender of the objectivity of morals might reasonably raise a two-fold objection to this picture. First he or she may reasonably question the extent to which moral judgement can be codified by principles which specify non-moral properties as the ground of these judgements. Often it takes moral judgement to discern that two cases are relevantly similar for the purposes of moral judgement. 'Murder is wrong' delimits a class of actions by reference to its members sharing the moral quality of being murderous. It is a moot point how far that quality can be cashed in terms of non-moral ones. If not, then there is nothing for a 'preference' against murder to latch onto. We shall return to this point in Chapter 3. Second the objectivist can contend that typically the desire to pursue the good and avoid the bad in any particular case is evoked by the judgement of moral reality and is unintelligible without that judgement. The desire presents itself to consciousness as called forth by the character of the circumstances. This fits in readily with our thought that moral education is a training in what to desire and hate as much as it is a training in the natural, or physical facts surrounding human choices. Desire presents itself as a cognitive state. Only the thought of desire as called forth in the recognition of an act's moral quality will adequately explain the overridingness of moral judgements. For on a non-cognitivist account of desire 'Moral judgements override' is either a miserable tautology or a happy but highly contingent fact. It is the former if it just means that we shall call those preferences of an agent 'moral' if they are overriding for him or her (but then are there no limits as to what someone might prefer above other things?). It is the latter if people just happen to have overriding preferences to heed the claims of universal, impartial right. (Point one in this reply is explored at length in Brennan 1977 and McNaughton 1988, point two in Dent 1984 and McNaughton 1988.)

Because the objectivist sees moral desire or preference as a cognitive state, he can accept much of what fact-value theorists have written about the distinctive qualities of language used in moral contexts without concluding that these accounts say anything important about the justification of moral judgements. To say that something is courageous, cruel, wrong, good and so forth may be to express attitudes, register commitments to action and evince feelings. Only if we, tendentiously, assume that cognitive and affective states are exclusive do important consequences follow from this for our account of moral truth. Rejecting this opposition between cognitive and affective judgements, we may accept that speech acts other than stating are performed in moral discourse without qualms. (Compare my words to the student: 'You are a careless scholar'. This condemns as well describes, expresses feelings as well as states a fact: see Bambrough 1979:21 ff.)

The opposition between cognition and desire is at the heart of the allegation of a fact-value distinction and of projectionist theories of value. This opposition is summed up in the dictum: 'No ought is entailed by an is'. It would take to long to unscramble what is acceptable and unacceptable in this slogan for the objectivist. In essence it would divide all moral judgement into recognition of natural properties and expression of attitude or preference to such properties. It is a thesis which stands or falls therefore with the other parts of the case for saying that a belief element in moral judgement can be separated from a desire element. It is not an independent, logical truth which proves the projectionist theory of value.

The objectivist has a ready source of examples which appear to refute the thesis that no ought follows from an is. They in turn question the projectionist account of value and the opposition between cognition and desire. The examples stem from the 'norms of reason'.

Illustrations are: 'If an argument is invalid, it cannot be relied on', 'If two propositions are inconsistent, one of them must be abandoned', 'If you see that one of your beliefs is false, you must give it up'. Here we have 'oughts' and 'musts' about what is to be said, done and believed following quite neatly from 'is' statements about the character of and relations between propositions. In the recognition of the claims of reason on belief and inference, we have cognition of the objective qualities of propositions, beliefs and arguments giving rise in itself to action. The claims for the opposition between belief and desire, cognition and action, fact and value do not appear to be universally true (see Edgely 1969 for a full discussion of the norms of reason).

What the objectivist wants is a proof positive that the apparent cognitivity of morals is an illusion.

2

Conscience, Moral Experience and Moral Theory

THE IDEA OF CONSCIENCE

The remainder of my argument will be based on the assumption that a cognitivist account of morality is correct and hence that there is such a thing as moral knowledge. Granted that there is something called 'moral knowledge', the questions arise: How do we acquire it? How is it constituted? If answers to these questions can be developed, then the assumption that there is such knowledge will be supported.

A traditional answer to the question as to how we acquire moral knowledge is 'Through conscience'. The idea of conscience as the seat of the individual's knowledge of right and wrong is linked to the phenomena of conscience: conscience invites us to do acts before our plans are set, witnesses our acts as we perform them, and accuses/excuses our conduct after action is complete. The phenomena of conscience testify to the apparent ability of all of us to refer future, present and past conduct to informed judgement of the good and the right. This presumed ability is what enables us to feel comfortable with the universal character of moral judgements and to hold all accountable for the moral worth of their actions. The existence of conscience appears to be the basis of the moral autonomy of each normal individual. Each is capable of being a judge of the correctness of his or her own actions. Each possesses a moral intellect which is free and independent of reliance on any authority. Conscience enables each person to function as a moral agent and to be held responsible for his or her actions in consequence.

21

Our traditional answer to the question of the source of knowledge of right and wrong is not incorrect, but it is incomplete and liable to be misleading in two respects: first in leading to the personification and isolation of the moral intellect, and second in suggesting that moral knowledge depends in its constitution on general knowledge and a theoretical account of the good and the right.

The personification of conscience arises naturally out of the tendency to seek a thing which the noun 'conscience' names and is encouraged by our talk of conscience 'warning', 'advising', 'admonishing' us and the like. So we may be tempted to think of it as an invisible monitor at our elbow, informing and encouraging us in the practice of virtue (see Kirk 1933:52). As Kenneth Kirk notes this is consistent with the personification we give to other principles of action in our lives. Prudence, honour, caution may likewise be spoken of as telling us this, dictating that we do that (1933:53). Such harmless metaphors may become vicious if they are seriously taken to imply that there is a separate faculty which is the human conscience. In that case, we are led to see conscience as somehow how separate from the self that it is connected to. If it is viewed as an added extra tacked onto the human self, talk of conscience clouds our understanding of the moral intellect. We may be encouraged to view the self as at best essentially amoral, or worst of all, immoral. It takes a distinct entity to see and acknowledge the moral truth – left alone the self has no inclination to see and pursue the good and the right. Personifying language of this sort might suggest that the self is the helpless plaything or battle-ground of forces over which it has no control. So: desire pulls it one way, conscience another. But such a picture leaves totally unclear how an agent's choice of a course of conduct in the face of competing considerations can be his or hers: something which he or she has decided upon and is accountable for (Nowell Smith 1954:263–4). Above all conscience as a separate faculty invites the thought that moral knowledge is acquired differently and independently of other forms of knowledge. We learn facts and principles of judgement about non-moral matters in the course of ordinary experience and education but a separate faculty (perhaps specially stocked with innate or God-given principles) is required for moral knowledge. It should, I shall insist, be a requirement of any account of moral knowledge that it allows such knowledge to be acquired through the same intellect that acquires other forms of knowledge and to be possessed by people who in general, and in relation to non-moral matters, are reasoning, thinking beings.

If conscience is not to be viewed as a separate faculty, it is best seen as just another way of referring to the capacity for reflective moral awareness possessed by adult, normally intelligent human beings as such. Given that we want to take the universality of moral judgement seriously and that we do not want to make a metaphysical mystery out of the process of acquiring and exercising moral knowledge, we ought to be able to explain how reflective moral awareness arises out of normal experience. In particular, reflective moral awareness arises from the experiences of a normal human life, including the experience, exercised in action, of making moral choices. Conscience reflects the normally developed human intellect's experience of moral choice. This is the surest foundation for belief in the capacity of all human beings to be autonomous moral agents.

These thoughts should make us initially sceptical of another widespread thought associated with conscience. Much of our talk about conscience likens its operation to the application of rules or principles to proposed, current or past courses of conduct. This would suggest that reflective moral awareness consists essentially in a knowledge of a body of legislation which when brought to bear on specific practical problems yields answers about how to act. We come to have moral knowledge only in so far as we have been given or learnt such a body of legislation. Moral knowledge is then at heart knowledge of rules and principles. This thought may lead us to conclude that the individual conscience is not fully informed unless it is acquainted with a moral theory. Such a theory would consist in a systematised body of rules and principles, in which a general account of the good and the right would be found. Systematisation implies an order and ranking of rules and principles: with a few very general first principles leading on to a greater number of less general ones, down to the manifold specific rules which govern right living. The kind of ordering and ranking we find in a collection of laws structured as in a theory appears to be a mark of perfection in a body of legislation. Only with this structure can we deduce from many rules and principles what to do if two or more of them clash in a particular case, or know whether a new rule is a good candidate for a admission into our corpus. All this suggests that moral knowledge is fundamentally of rules and principles and that its basis is theoretical. A fully informed conscience would possess a theory of right and wrong. Finally, this points to one role for philosophy in morals. Many moral philosophers have seen their task as that of providing a moral theory, that is a statement and systematic ordering of the primary principles of morality. In that case, it would take moral philosophy to complete the informing of conscience. Moral philosophy would play a vital role in the settling of practical dilemmas, because it would contain the highest form of moral knowledge: the key principles from which the rest is derived and ordered.

I believe this picture of the nature and basis of moral knowledge and of the role of moral philosophy to be profoundly mistaken. I shall offer in its place a view which holds that moral knowledge arises out of making specific moral choices and of our experience of concrete human relationships. Human life is moral in its very form and moral knowledge is exercised and acquired in the most basic transactions of human living. This is to suggest that we do not make choices, express and acquire preferences and, *post facto*, see if these amount to moral knowledge by applying rules and principles to them. It is to suggest that modes of choice, preference and relationship to others already embody moral knowledge. Negatively, my thesis questions the extent to which moral knowledge can be summed up in knowledge of rule and principle. Positively, it affirms the extent to which specific choices contain and constitute forms of moral knowledge. If these two halves of my view are correct then moral theory is at best an addition to conscience and not its basis. Correspondingly, there is only a limited role for moral philosophy in the shaping of moral knowledge.

The negative part of my thesis about moral theory rests upon the simple but powerful point that the application of any moral principle or rule to a particular case is itself something that demands moral knowledge and skill. This suggests two further things: first that the entire content of moral knowledge cannot be expressed in terms of rules and principles, and second that rules and principles may play only a limited role in summing up moral knowledge.

Moral rules are of at least two kinds. Some attach right or wrong to act-types which are picked out in morally neutral fashion. 'Truth telling is right' would be an example of such a rule. Others pick out classes of act in terms of their morally relevant features. 'Murder is wrong' would be an example of such a rule. Now there may be no great effort of discrimination involved in deciding when a rule of the first type is applicable to a set of circumstances. However, such rules notoriously yield morally insensitive behaviour if they are regarded as determining without further moral judgement whether acts are licit or illicit. Granted that I know that my proposed act would be one of 'telling the truth', what moral reason is interested in is whether it is right to tell the truth on this occasion. While the requirement to tell the truth may be a decisively relevant consideration on one occasion, it my be comparatively irrelevant on other occasions. It may be overridden by other more decisive considerations (such as the the need to respect confidences or not to give gratuitous offence). It takes moral judgement and discernment to decide on the relevance and importance of qualities picked out by moral rules of this first type. What such judgement needs is a faithfulness to the detailed circumstances of any particular occasion of choice, a faithfulness which would be ruled out by too great a reliance on rules of this first sort.

If I condemn an act as wrong because murderous, I am not judging it wrong because it fits some class which can be initially picked out in a morally neutral fashion. All murders are homicides, but not all homicides are murders. Nor are murders homicides of a certain morally neutral kind to which moral condemnation is then attached. Murders are homicides for which the normal justifications of homicides do not apply. We have a general principle that 'Homicide is a heinous act which is wrong unless strongly justified'. This suggests more specific rules: 'Do not kill/do not murder'. But whether the rule forbidding killing is to be obeyed in a particular case, or whether the rule outlawing murder applies in that case, depends on the exercise of moral judgement. One who has the ability to judge whether acts are alike in being acts of murder has the skill to judge of the morally relevant similarities of acts and their circumstances (compare Brennan 1977:41ff). No one can be given that skill by being made acquainted with a rule which cashes out those morally relevant similarities in terms of physical or natural categories. This would be to deny what someone skilled in the ethics of homicide possesses: namely moral discernment and judgement, something which can only be the fruit of experience and reflection. This reinforces the point made in Chapter 1 that moral judgements cannot be analysed into an element of descriptive meaning referring to physical or natural properties plus an element of evaluation.

The essence of my negative thesis can be summed up as follows: moral knowledge cannot adequately be expressed in terms of rules and principles because it takes moral knowledge to judge of the applicability and force of rules and principles. An implicit contrast is being drawn in this argument between the way reason operates on morality and in the sciences. No one would say when faced with working out the trajectory of a falling object: 'let us not rely on the laws of motion but patiently discern the unique features of this particular case'. Science can treat justly of varied phenomena through general principles because it depends on a a highly abstractive use of reason. It can thus rely on highly general principles in judging of the relevant similarities between cases. Its success in so doing reflects on the fundamental properties of physical reality. Equally, the different way in which intelligent reason must operate in morals reflects on the fundamental features of the meaning and significance possessed by human acts and their circumstances.

My thesis is not intended to be a form of irrationalism. I am concerned to give an account of the way in which reason operates in morals. On this ground I wish to distinguish it from two other approaches which may appear similar: intuitionism and situationalism. Intuitionism favoured by English moral philosophers between the Wars smacks of the notion that moral principles are self-evidently true, and just have to be seen to be so, without argument. Or it implies the possession of a mysterious capacity to discern, immediately and non-discursively, a range of 'non-natural properties' in acts (for a fuller account see Warnock 1967:4–17). Situationalism may appear to have similar emphases to my account. However, it displays irrationalist tendencies with characteristic appeals to 'love' to find the answer to moral dilemmas where appeals to rules fail. As has been pointed out before, appeals to love as our moral guide are either empty or indicative of the wrong-headed notion that it matters not what we do, provided that we act out of a good motive (MacIntyre 1967:71–2). Neither intuitionism nor situationalism promises a good account of moral knowledge, for neither appears to offer a picture of how moral discernment can be learnt and how its deliverances can be argued over.

If there is reason in morality then there is argument. And argument is bound by the formal requirement of all argument, namely to reach similar conclusions about similar cases. Neither intuitionism nor situationalism promises to honour these requirements. If I judge an act to be wrong, I am committed to judging wrong any relevantly similar act in relevantly similar circumstances. 'Relevant' here means 'morally relevant'. But how am I to reason about that without any strict rules to guide me? The answer to this question is given in the writings of F. R. Leavis and John Wisdom (see Byrne 1979) and consists in appeal to reasoning through 'placing' arguments (Leavis) or through 'case by case procedure' (Wisdom). The truth that a given act is a wrongful violation of the rule 'Tell the truth', a case of unmitigated deceit, cannot be settled by reference to the natural or physical facts of the act alone, nor can it always be settled by appeal to rules. Two individuals may agree about the facts and, at least notionally, on what rules are relevant to the case but still dispute the morality of the act. What they disagree over is the interpretation and significance of the facts. In the absence of principles whose relevance and interpretation is agreed, reasoning may proceed by appeal to parallel cases. The parties would need to find admitted cases of unjustified withholding of truth. They would each try to show how like and unlike their disputed case was to these. This can proceed by exhibiting or constructing parallel intermediate cases, and by presenting contrasting examples where not telling the whole truth is justified. To see their disputed case as a rightful departure from the rule of veracity is to see is as like and unlike a range of other acts. It is to place it in a map of agreed judgements on how to see departures from truth telling. The details of the case and of the larger map are there to be examined and conveyed in one way or another by way of establishing the place of this disputed case on the map.

This is argument and it shows the exercise of reason. The measure of its success is agreement. It can distinguish between real and phoney agreement: if our parties have come to a genuine, shared insight that this is unjustified deceit then have found rather than invented a relevant moral similarity between this case and others. This will entail that they will be able to non-collusively agree on yet other cases in the same area. If they don't, their agreement on the case that started the argument was not genuine and did not serve to confirm them in the possession of insight. Someone might object that this reliance on human agreement shows that reasoning through case-by-case procedure is fatally flawed. In truly rational enquiries reasoning starts from admitted principles and is validated as correct by appeal to such principles. But appeal to principles to begin the work of reason and to judge its final success is only appeal to human agreement by another route. To get underway all argument requires a common starting point, be it a common principle or a common judgement about a particular case. If we end an argument by validating its conclusion by reference to a principle, the matter is settled only if that principle is agreed upon. Moreover, both principles used at the start and end of the work of argument are only of use in their respective tasks if they are interpreted in the same way by those who participate in the work of reason. Whether they do interpret them in the same way depends in the end on whether they agree on specific facts or inferences that give rise to them or exemplify them. The meaning of a specific rule might be settled by a appeal to a further agreed rule, but whether minds really unite in that rule depends on whether it is interpreted in the same way. At the cost of starting a vicious infinite regress, agreement in principles has to resolve itself in agreement on particular instances which exemplify them. (This is the burden on Wittgenstein's brilliant discussion of following a rule: see Wittgenstein 1953:54–88.) We can now see a connection between case-by-case reasoning and reasoning in terms of rules and principles. They are not so opposed as we have pretended. John Wisdom points out the similarity thus:

> Examples are the final food of thought. Principles and laws may serve us well. They can help us to bring to bear on what is now in question what is not now in question. They help us to connect one thing with another and another. But at the bar of reason, always the final appeal is to cases. (Wisdom 1965:102)

These points should suffice to show that a commitment to reason in ethics is not the same as the commitment to theory in ethics. They also show how one fundamental requirement for any account of moral judgement can be met: moral judgement must be teachable. It is not unknown for defenders of theory in ethics to claim that without reliance on principles no one can know where a person's moral judgements are coming from: they will remain isolated, episodic judgements about individual cases with no bearing on other judgements and their grounds will remain ever mysterious. (These might be cogent criticisms of more extreme forms of situationalism.) But our account shows that one can know where someone's judgements are coming from without essential or close reliance on rules: they may stem from a way of ordering a range of cases and embody judgements of moral likeness and unlikeness between cases. In the best instances they will embody a pattern of discernment. A pattern of discernment can be teachable. (Just as I can teach someone the difference between the appearance in winter of slavonian and black-necked grebes: non-bird watchers be assured rules are of some use in making this discrimination but they rapidly give out and are no substitute for the practised eye.) Indeed our account points to a general picture of moral education. It will consist in passing on discernment and judgement, not only or mainly through the inculcation of rules, but through training in the making of discriminations between particular cases and the passing on of techniques in attending to the morally relevant features of those cases. It is the passing on of a communicable vision, not skill in the operation of a calculus (McNaughton 1988:204–5).

MORAL KNOWLEDGE AND MORAL EXPERIENCE

I have implied something of my positive account of the sources of moral knowledge in presenting criticisms of the reliance on theory in ethics. My account can only work if it is the case that there are sources of moral knowledge prior to awareness of moral theory and its components. This is indeed implied in Aristotle's account of the building blocks of moral thought in the *Nicomachean Ethics*.

Consider what Aristotle says about how one might become a just man or woman: 'we become just by doing just acts' (Aristotle 1925a:1103ᵃ). Virtues are acquired by repetition of the corresponding acts. But this implies that no one is made just by being taught a principle, for example 'Justice is giving to each his or her due'. To be just is to be capable of making choices of a certain sort. It is the ability to see what is owing to others and the ability to act upon that knowledge. It is a species of practical knowledge. We can acquire such knowledge through repeated performance of acts on the assumption that such acts involve skills of judgement and discrimination. I must be exercising such skills in the making of individual choices if through repeated exercise of choice I am to acquire a knowledge of justice. I am trained in the performance of rudimentary just acts and in the exercise of primitive choices for justice, and from that basis make further acts of choice through which my knowledge of what justice consists in increases. I learn what is choiceworthy through making choices.

This gives us a picture of moral knowledge as flowing upward from acts of choice to more general and abstract expressions of that knowledge. Making moral choices itself embodies and inculcates moral knowledge. Aristotle's general picture of the relation of principles to conclusions in ethics confirms this. Ethics is a science where the first principles derive from experience (1925a:1142a). Expertise and experience concerning the objects of experience (here, choices and what they aim at) is required to understand any principles that experience suggests, hence his claim that young men should not attempt to study moral philosophy (1925a:1095a). Principles are not expunged from ethical enquiry but in the order of knowledge they come second after acts of intelligent choice. If we search, as Aristotle says we must, for a generalised good for humankind which will be the ultimate object of intelligent choice it is not because without knowledge of that object we shall not know what is worth choosing at all. Rather it will give us a mark to aim at, the better to direct skills we already have (1925a:1094a).

In developing a positive account of how moral knowledge is built up we must avoid supposing that moral choice is the expression of non-rational preferences which are attached to independently discernible patterns of similarity and difference in the natural and physical qualities of actions and their circumstances. Nor must we suppose that we have knowledge of natural facts and then add to this further knowledge of a body of moral rules and principles which gives us moral opinions. Rather we must be capable of discerning the dimension of moral significance in the world just in making choices. We must be capable of perceiving what is proper, fitting and good in the simple business of learning how to make choices between courses of conduct. Our preferences then come to embody a knowledge of these things. Morality is not then a doctrine laid on top of untutored or unreasoned preference. As theoretically expressed it is making explicit a knowledge of what is right and wrong, good and bad in choices where this knowledge exists prior to those choices. Some recent writings of Bernard Harrison bring out *one* way in which this might be so (Harrison 1984 and 1989). They give one way of defending the thought that the normal experience of life is a morally ordered experience, giving rise to moral knowledge. Human life is moral in form and it is out of the experience of a normal human life that conscience arises.

The manner in which human life is moral in form according to Harrison may be summed up as follows. The activities and ends of a normal life are impossible without a range of relationships to others. These relationships are constituted by: forms of mutual trust, conventions which structure that trust, and a willingness to abide by claims arising out of these trust conventions (Harrison 1984:314 and 311–12). An example to illustrate Harrison's thesis would be the relationship of friendship. Two individuals cannot stand in the relation of friend to friend unless they tacitly accept that certain conventions govern their conduct toward one another. The conventions give shape to the kind of trust that constitutes friendship. To acknowledge these conventions and be governed by the form of trust required is to be ready to accept the force of certain claims that can be made if actions of either party appear to violate these trust conventions. If two people become companions, begin to share time together and to pursue mutual interests, yet one openly acts against the other's interests at the first occasion of any conflict, then the question will arise of whether they were ever really friends. If the offender can see no force in the claims for redress and apology which his conduct naturally gives rise to, then they were not related as friends. One party just happens to have found it useful to be and work with another in the pursuit of his or her own interests and pleasures. He or she has never been willing to give or receive the kind of trust than makes two people friends. He or she has never been willing to modify concern for his or her own interests in the light of the claims of friendship, such willingness being characteristic of being someone's friend.

We have, according to Harrison, the power to acquire 'reciprocal extended personal interests' through our capacity and willingness to enter into such forms of moral relationship with others (Harrison 1989:310). To enter into a moral relationship of the kind delineated is to see the sphere of one's own private interests merged with those of others. In our paradigm case of friendship a mark of accepting the conventions that govern and constitute the relationship is that I be ready to accept the demands that the other's interests make upon my conduct and concerns. If I have no willingness to let the other's interests count as my own, I am not that person's genuine friend, no matter how long my conduct simulates friendship or pursuit of my interests coincides with desire to enjoy his or her companionship and cooperation.

All manner of ways of being related to others are constituted by forms of trust between human beings. They are then impossible unless those involved are prepared to acknowledge the claims of others in the ways appropriate to such relationships. The pursuit of our most basic and characteristic ends is bound up in the forms of social life that these moral relationship make possible. We do not have ends or preferences and then ask what morality tells us about the permissible ways in which we might pursue them. A vast range of our interests would be unintelligible unless we were related to others as friend to friend, partners in a business enterprise, parent to child, pupil to teacher, fellow citizens pursuing the national interest, fellow competitors in a sport. Our life is therefore inescapably shot through with an awareness of moral claims upon our conduct and the recognition of the interests of others as things which demand our respect. The level of moral significance in actions and their surrounding circumstances is perceptible to us just in virtue of our capacity and readiness to enter into forms of relationship with other human beings.

To realise the force of these points consider what kind of human life is possible to one who cannot trust others and offer to be trusted in turn. Young Blitzer in Dickens' *Hard Times* has learnt the lessons of Gradgrind's philosophy well: 'the whole social system is a question self-interest'. So when an appeal is made to his 'heart' to consider another in distress and avoid taking personal advantage out of that distress, his reply expresses incomprehension at what is being suggested: 'What you must always appeal to is a person's self-interest. It is your only hold' (Dickens 1969:303). In one sense Blitzer's actions can be trusted – in the way that I can trust my car to start each morning. His behaviour is predictable. We know he will always act upon a rational calculation of his own interest. He may also in this sense trust others: either to act, as he would have it, fool-ishly and sentimentally (in so far as they have not seen the basis of 'the whole social system'), or to pursue their own self-interest under the 'mask' of moral relationships. But no one could repose trust in him where this involved seeing him as ready to acknowledge the claims of others in relationship or to feel the interests of others as if they were his own. And thinking morality a sham, he no doubt will not repose this kind of trust in others. The range of his interests will have to be limited so as to exclude any inextricable merging of his own interests with others' or the pursuit of things which can only be attained through submerging one's self in a larger concern (for example furthering the good of a cooperative enterprise, such as a nation or college). Any pursuit, project or relationship which threatens his ability to keep his interests clearly separate from others also threatens to ruin his philosophy. He must have a clear criterion of what are his interests, as opposed to those of others, to make his rational egoism possible. But it is just characteristic of being someone's genuine friend, parent, fellow researcher, partner and the like that this clear separation cannot be made. Blitzer and those who know him will realise that he will only go along with the claims of relationships for as long as this suits interests of his which are fixed prior to entering into them and which remain unaffected by them. What then is he able to pursue? What possibilities of living lie open for him? The answer to these questions which appears most obvious is this: a very limited range of goals and a very impoverished form of human life. The range of interests he can have and the range of things that might move him appear very thin indeed. If Blitzer's project were to be consistently carried through and he never offered trust to, or placed placed trust in, another, never allowed his interests to be extended by genuine concern for the interests of another, his life would be so limited in its sources of satisfaction, its goals, its motives as to make more than rhetorical the question 'Is this a form of human life at all?' (compare Harrison 1984:316–17.)

Harrison's arguments have the merit of showing the depth from which the roots of morality spring. We have to be aware of and be prepared to be guided by a range of moral conventions which define forms of trust and respect between persons in order in turn to be able to enter into a large range of human relationships. An ability to enter into these relationships is a condition for having a large proportion of the goals we pursue and of living a recognizably human form of existence. This shows, in part, why moral knowledge is not primarily theoretical, and why we have moral knowledge just in virtue of being normal, adult human beings. It also hints at deficiencies in the doctrine of the fact/value distinction. The facts relevant to much moral judgement are not made relevant because we apply preferences to them. They are moral in their import, because they arise out of the moral form of human life. Our awareness of the circumstances of human living is all but inevitably one of a morally significant world. (Consider here the difficulties Blitzer must face in comprehending the behaviour of others and of avoiding using any moral categories to inform his own motives and self-understanding.)

The move to make moral knowledge dependent on a moral theory can now be seen to mistaken, at least as far as some moral knowledge is concerned. One particular way of introducing the idea of moral theory is to be avoided. According to a thesis defended by John Rawls among others (Rawls 1972:19–21) it should be the goal of a rational account of moral knowledge to provide a theory which will show how our 'moral intuitions' (that is judgements about specific rights and wrongs) follow from as few a number of general principles as possible. Ideally, too, those few principles should be ranked in order of importance and priority. The analogy for reconstructing moral thought rationally is the logician's attempt to show how our intuitions about the validity of inferences flow from a few principles of logic, down through more specific rules of deduction. Moral philosophy, naturally, has the job of rationally reconstituting moral knowledge in this theoretical mould. Just as in the case of logic's attempts to order our knowledge of valid inference, our intuitions about right and wrong will be modified in the process. We will through discovery of plausible rules and principles come to see that some intuitions are inconsistent with others. Those which appear to be stronger we will retain. The weaker will be abandoned. In this fashion, intuitions will guide the selection of rules and principles and they will in turn guide the selection of which intuitions are to be retained. The process is complete when philosophy establishes a reflective equilibrium between intuition and principle.

I consider this picture of the task of moral philosophy in relation to moral experience to be seriously misleading, at best. Key criticisms are listed below.

1.   Talk of moral intuitions implies that ground level moral judgements are guesses or hunches only achieving the status of judgement or knowledge when integrated into a theoretical structure. This is wrong. Our previous discussions indicate that they should be viewed more on the lines of perceptual judgements. They are expressions of discernment and the vision of moral qualities. They are of course defeasible and corrigible like all such judgements, but they are not blank intuitions.

2.   Given the above point and other arguments of this chapter, there is always likely to be more in a moral judgement than can be expressed in a formal rule or principle. If sound, judgement is the expression of discernment. We must be concerned with consistency between specific moral judgements, but this may not be established easily by asking if the same rule is behind two apparently conflicting judgements. The account of

case-by-case reasoning shows that we might have to establish consistency by other methods.

3. If particular moral judgements embody, where valid, discernment and vision, it may be idle to ask what principles, at some given moment, would give ordered expression to those judgements. As discernment moral judgement is always capable of refinement. We would be morally stupid to to take stock of our 'intuitions' at one moment and see what principles would unite them together. There is in any case no reason to suppose that moral philosophers have more moral discernment than others. Their typical background and the record of their forays into 'practical ethics' does not suggest that they are morally more wise than others. There is considerable merit in Aristotle's suggestion that it is not possible to practically wise without moral virtue (Aristotle 1925a:1144[a-b]). Such wisdom is an achievement of virtue.

4. Could not discernment be promoted by awareness of rule and principle? It might, but that depends on the case. Principles and rules are an aid to thought, as John Wisdom notes (see above). In some cases it takes substantial moral discernment to see what the import of a proposed principle or rule comes to. The authority of a principle in ethics may, as Bernard Williams notes, depend not on the theory of which it is a part but on its being seen to implied by specific moral judgement (Williams 1985:111).

5. Finally, our confidence in the ability of the philosophical enterprise of reconstructing moral knowledge according to Rawls' pattern is weakened by one important fact noted by Williams: it is a goal of such theories to show how moral judgement follows from as few principles and key concepts as possible (Williams 1985:116–7). But as Williams further argues, it is *prima facie* odd to suppose that all our varied moral discriminations can be shown to flow from the grasp and application of a few very general concepts; and it would be odd to argue that we make too many moral discriminations or that we should make do with fewer key concepts to guide is in our manifold discriminations. The drive to theory is a drive to economy and abstraction. Granted that these goals are proper and fitting in other areas of human enquiry, the question is: how far, if at all, should morality be seen as an appropriate sphere to pursue them?

MORAL RULES AND MORAL THEORIES

In defending the idea that the *major* sources of moral knowledge and conscience do not lie in theory we have met two ideas that allow us to see *some* positive role for theoretical insight in moral knowledge. We have argued that moral thought must recognise the basic requirements of consistency and universalisability that govern all rational modes of thought, and we have argued against the tendency to reduce the resources of moral thought. Rules and principles are one resource of moral thought which it would be stupid to reject entirely. Moral rules and principles enable us to sum up knowledge of the character of a multiciplicity of moral cases and therefore to bring to bear what we have established about one case with what we must decide about another. They also enable us to connect moral judgement with larger beliefs about the character of the world we experience.

I am not suggesting that the informed conscience should not approach questions about the licitness of homicide armed with the rule 'Murder is wrong'. This expresses a genuine insight. It affirms that acts of homicide are illicit unless justified and expresses our sense that an act of unjustified homicide is peculiarly and deeply evil. It is not a rule which can tell us in mechanical fashion which acts of of homicide are unjustified as homicides. It is an expression of moral judgement rather than a substitute for it. But its evocation of a general moral category is an aid to judgement in the individual case. The way the rule that murder is not to be done operates in moral thought shows that general principles are involved in it, in particular the principle that taking human life is a great harm that requires the most strenuous justification. That principle will in turn connect with larger considerations about why human life should be seen as having great value and what kind of circumstances might negate respect for that value. Here we can readily acknowledge that answers to such questions will be influenced by wider considerations which will mark points at which moral judgement shows itself to be in part embedded in different pictures of human nature and human circumstances. Such pictures are in need of exploration and can properly the subject of argument and debate. A properly worked out conception of the value of human life would indeed help to anchor and guide the moral discriminations we make about licit and illicit homicides. Moreover, we might hope that these more general levels of moral thought could help us to sort out the clashes that will inevitably arise between lower level moral rules.

Moral thought that is theoretical in form can be seen as an aid to greater reflectiveness and consistency in moral judgement. Seeing it in this light does not negate the contentions that conscience is formed by moral judgements on specific cases and that conscientious human choices in themselves constitute a form of knowledge about how to act. General principles and more specific rules will still require moral judgement to be applied. The content of principle can be informed as much by what sense judgement can make of particular cases as by generalising thought about human nature and circumstances. Some forms of generalising thought will be judged false by reference to the very fact that they do not square with conscientious human choices. We should always be wary of concluding from the fact that a given judgement can be shown to be implied by a principle that therefore the principle justifies the judgement. For often the principles we appeal to in moral thought have less certainty than the judgements they invite us to make. The final test any scheme of moral principles will be the sense it makes of the moral life and the choices that must be made in it. This is only proper, given that ethics is a practical science.

So we should see the sense and strength of our knowledge that murder is wrong as coming from two complementary sources. One is thought about what makes human life valuable and what considerations might justify taking it. Another is conscientious judgement about occasions of homicide. Our thought here moves in dialectical, spiral fashion. Judgements beget general notions to make sense of them. General notions beget further, revised and new judgements. The attempt to make those judgements conscientiously begets further, revised and new notions, which in turn beget further judgements, and so on. Moral thought shows itself here to be a process. It is a process which contains knowledge, because it is one which establishes discriminations between particular cases. Many things, including some very abstract and general modes of thought, contribute to the process. But the process is never complete. No final statement of abstract, unifying notions is attained; no final balance between the abstract and the concrete parts of the spiral is ever achieved. Both the internal dynamics of the process and the fact that life forces ever fresh circumstances of choice upon us rule this out.

Granted that there is some role for moral theory in the process of moral thought, we can (following Dent 1984:31–4) distinguish three types of theory propogated in the history of moral philosophy: consequentialist, deontological, and aretaic. Each of these theories promises a different account of the basis on which discriminations between right and wrong acts can be made, and focuses on a different aspect of human action in so doing.

Consequentialist moral theories focus on the desirable and undesirable consequences flowing from human acts as their chief or only right-making characteristic. It promotes an ultimate moral principle which bids us to maximise the desirable results of action and minimise the undesirable results. Facets of actions other than their projected consequences (desirable and undesirable) are dismissed as morally irrelevant or allowed to be relevant only in so far as they have an indirect bearing on these consequences. Deontological moral theories have as their core an account of the basic moral rules. These rules are the foundations of our discriminations between right and wrong. They tend to focus on the inherent nature of acts as this nature is fixed by the intentions of those who perform them. The intentions behind acts enables them to be placed into moral kinds, which are then judged obligatory, forbidden or permissible according to the moral rules which deontological moral theory aims to discover and justify. Aretaic moral theories have as their chief focus an account of the virtues of the morally excellent human being. They are theories about the content of such virtues and about how possession and knowledge of the virtues generates moral knowledge and principles of choice. A right act for such a theory is roughly one which would be performed by the good human being or the doing of which would be part of the good life. The good person and the good life are defined in terms of the possession and display of the human virtues. So such theories further identify a right act as one which would reflect or embody in its principle of choice one or more of the virtues. They tend then to focus on the motive of an act as its chief right-making characteristic.

These theories then give us: three accounts of the obligatory nature of an action; three sources or foci for a theory of ethics; and three aspects of action to consider as contributing to its rightness and goodness (consequences, intention and motive). These theories will provide the subject matter for much of our remaining discussion. Though I shall consistently present them as rivals we must note that they could all be accepted as contributing to a full portrait of the sources of moral knowledge, because, perhaps, all three aspects of action are important in determining its moral character and none can be reduced to the others. Before commenting in detail on this question, we shall need to explore in greater detail the anatomy of action.

One of the major considerations we must bring to bear on these theories is how far they allow us to keep the picture of moral knowledge built up so far. If any one of them promises to respect better than the others the structure of conscience that we have outlined, it will, other things being equal, be superior to its rivals. If we engage in the pursuit of a moral theory we must look, paradoxically, for one which explains how all moral knowledge is not theoretical.

3
The Moral Structure of Action

THE ANATOMY OF ACTION

The purpose of this chapter is to explore the moral structure of the human act. Thereby we may gain a clearer grasp of the moral relevance of the various factors which contribute to an act's goodness or rightness. In the course of this exploration the starting points of the different types of moral theory that we have distinguished will become clearer and a number of key questions in moral philosophy and moral theology will be addressed.

Good discussions of the moral anatomy of action are hard to find. The basis of my treatment will be a survey of St Thomas Aquinas' account of these matters in the *Summa Theologiae* 1a 2ae Questions 18–21 (Aquinas 1966a). In many respects his treatment remains the best available, and though I do not offer my discussion of him as in any sense a true interpretation of his intentions, his account can be used to introduce, explain and discuss all the main distinctions and issues relevant to the topic. After setting out an anatomy of action based loosely on Aquinas' words various important critical questions about the moral appraisal of action will be considered in turn.

Aquinas' account provides a basis of for the three-fold analysis of the morally relevant parts of action that we found in Dent. Thus we have:

i.   The nature of the act itself determined by its objective (or intention).
ii.   The end of the act (or motive).
iii.   The circumstances of the act (or consequences).

Aquinas in fact teaches that there are four features of a human act that are relevant to its moral worth. In addition to the above three, there is its 'real quality as an action' (1966a:19), by which he means the notion that all acts just in being voluntary performances of a rational creature have a measure of goodness or worth. Acts, as distinct from mere behaviour or bodily movement, embody choice and intention, and thus reason to some degree. Though in this minimal sense all intentional human performances have some worth, we can quickly forget this aspect of worth, for since it is present in all acts in so far as they are acts at all it is of no relevance to the task of distinguishing between which acts are choiceworthy and which are not. What is significant about this fourth, universal feature of acts as acts is that it points to Aquinas' thesis that what makes an act good tends also to complete its full reality as an act. An act is distinguished from mere behaviour or movement because it embodies reason (in the form of purpose and intention). When its other three, variable elements – objective, end and circumstance – are fully in accord with reason then it becomes a good act and thus attains its full reality as a human act, that is: a bodily performance embodying reason. We will meet the thought that the perfection of action relates to its nature as rational performance again in Chapter 6.

Aquinas contends that, in general, goodness in a human act is due to an integrity of all of its features: it is good when all three features distinguished contribute out of their individual goodness to the goodness of the whole. There is thus an asymmetry between goodness and evil in action: 'each single defect causes evil, whereas complete integrity is required for good' (1966a:19). Aquinas is right to set before us an ideal for good action: one in which we seek to have all elements of action adjusted in the light of reason. However, the doctrine that failure in one element of action makes action evil is over-strenuous, unrealistic and probably inconsistent with things he affirms elsewhere. Once we allow that the goodness or rightness of an act may be a matter of degree then the doctrine that all elements must be correct to have goodness in the whole is seen to be empty. Granted that perfection in a human act comes only when we have this complete integrity, we can see that an act whose circumstances, for example, are not morally ideal may nonetheless be choiceworthy, better than any alternatives and even morally obligatory. We may feel that it is very rare indeed that circumstances allow human choices to be made which have the 'complete integrity' that Aquinas' seeks. There may indeed be occasions when moral defect in one particular facet of action makes an act evil (that is, not choiceworthy, impermissible) while the other two features are correct in isolation. But it will not just be any defect in action which has the effect of marring the whole to this extent. Aquinas himself, as we shall see, pays special attention to wrongness in the objective as something which might make an act forbidden, regardless of goodness in the end and circumstances, thus showing that he does not altogether believe in the doctrine that a single defect anywhere in action makes for evil.

Drawing precise, clear distinctions between the morally relevant elements of action is not easy, as a discussion of Aquinas' distinction between objective and end will indicate.

By the objective of an act Aquinas means roughly what we would call in ordinary usage its intention. It is the end or purpose of the act specified in its customary description. So the objective of an act of stealing is to take what does not belong to you; of adultery to have carnal knowledge of person who is not your spouse; of lying to tell a deliberate falsehood; of homicide to kill a human being. Human acts embody purpose and intention. They are done for a reason. The objective of an act is the immediate intention or purpose embodied in it. It is that layer of intention which provides the most natural answer to the question 'What was he/she doing, what act was performed?'. The first requirement of a good act is then that its objective be in accordance with reason, that its immediate aim be reasonable (1966a: 11 and 21–23).

Aquinas' discussions on 17–19 and 25–7 show that he wants to distinguish the contribution of the objective to an act's goodness from that of its 'end'. The problem is that the objective of an act is also a species of end embodied in it. 'End' really refers to a distinct level of aim involved in action. The immediate intention of an act of stealing is to take what does not belong to one. One has not successfully stolen if that intention is not completed. But there might be different ends behind many acts all alike in being acts of stealing. And one might successfully accomplish an act of stealing even even if one's end in stealing is not achieved. A theft might have the ends of: helping the poor, hurting an enemy, making oneself rich. Aquinas' thought in distinguishing end from objective is that as well as an immediate purpose embodied in action there is commonly a more general, over-arching purpose behind that action. The notion of end roughly corresponds to one of the facets of purpose that we pick out by the word 'motive'. Aquinas himself indicates this connection between end and motive when he illustrates the 'end intended' in an act by the example of giving alms in order to show off (1966a:87). 'Showing off' would be a good example of a motive displayed in a specific act. So upon witnessing a lie we might say 'Yes I know that he lied, but what was his motive?' thereby requesting the general end for which the immediate purpose of communicating a falsehood was pursued. There can obviously be a variety of ends behind the pursuit of one objective; such ends can be judged appropriate or inappropriate in the light of standards of reasonableness and thus may add to or detract from the moral worth of an action.

We might think it easy to capture the distinction between objective/intention and end/motive by saying that the former answers the question 'What act was done?', while the latter answers the question 'Why was the act done?' The former supplies act-descriptions, the latter act-reasons or explanations. But this is much too simple. The intention in firing a revolver at someone's head may have been to kill him, while the motive may have been to destroy a tyrant. 'Destroying a tyrant' may be offered as a description of what is done, while at one level 'Trying to kill someone' answers the question 'Why was he firing that pistol?'. These points reflect the simple fact that acts may be described at different levels of specificity and reasons for action can be sought at different stages of a performance. Aquinas is surely right in distinguishing, as raising separate topics for moral discussion, the immediate from the more general purposes embodied in action and to imply that these layers of purpose have different relations to our classifications of actions.

It is worthwhile considering the legal doctrine that from the action you may infer the intention but not the motive. If we witness someone taking goods out of a shop without paying we may infer that, assuming he or she was aware of the basic facts surrounding the action, that what what was done had the intention or objective of stealing. The motive however is not so clearly revealed in the observable performance. Whether it was revenge, charity, self-agrandizement, political or whatever could only be discovered on uncovering a context of the agent's further beliefs, desires and personal circumstances. The purpose of taking what belongs to another is the first point at which the question of reasonableness might arise. (The agent as well as taking away property was also moving his legs and arms, but no question about reasonableness emerges at that level of description and the intent to move legs and arms was not a controlling feature of the action or present to consciousness. So we do not begin our act description or moral investigation there.) Further and different questions of reasonableness arise at Aquinas' level of ends, and because the nature of this dimension to the act cannot be inferred from performance itself there is reason to regard it as distinct from the intention behind 'the act itself'.

For Aquinas objectives/intentions provide a basic level of act description and classification, the first level at which moral questions arise and the basic categories of morally good, bad and indifferent kinds of acts. When considering the morality of acts, he states:

> the first relevant character is what provides a thing's specific character. As in a physical thing this is given by its form, so in an action this is given by the character of its objective. Hence . . . the basic goodness of a moral act is provided by the befitting objective in which it is set: hence some moralists refer to an act as being 'good of its kind' . . . the basic evil in moral acts arises from the objective, for instance to take what does not belong to you: then an act is referred to as being 'bad of its kind'. (1966a:9–11, translation slightly amended)

So from objectives we get species of acts, which give them a basic classification as good, bad or indifferent. These moral species are close to what E. D'Arcy refers to as 'moral case terms' (D'Arcy 1963:18ff) and Crombie as 'actions of a definite kind' (Crombie 1966:247). Examples of moral species are: giving to charity, lying stealing, killing. Two chief characteristics of such moral species make them apt to serve as the most basic way of classifying acts morally. First their quality as members of such species can be discerned without too much of the remoter significance of acts having to be taken into account (Crombie 1966:247). Objective/intention can be established without paying too much attention to end/motive or circumstances. Second the layer of intention in an act which makes it a member of such a species cannot be ignored, since it is the first level of genuine purpose which can be confronted with standards of reasonableness. Robin Hood may argue that his acts of theft are praiseworthy because done in order to help the poor, but he cannot contend that we should not describe them as thefts or that their character as members of the species 'stealing' is irrelevant to their moral character. Act-kinds can be formed out of words that refer primarily to motives/ends, but because ends as motives lack these two features they are not apt for the purpose of providing the most fundamental moral species.

Objectives give us moral species: classifications into kinds of act which are good, bad or indifferent. Aquinas' general teaching is that such classification begins the work of deciding whether individual acts are choiceworthy. If an act falls into a good species by virtue of its objective, consideration of its end and circumstance will establish whether it is finally good. If it falls into an evil species, end and circumstances may be considered in determining the degree of its evil. (Can they be such as to make an act evil of its species nonetheless right? There are complexities behind this question which must be considered below.) If the act's objective puts it in a class of indifferent acts then it will still have a moral character according to Aquinas (there being no acts which are morally indifferent in the individual case – 1966a:37). In this instance this will be wholly determined by its end and circumstances.

Objectives also give moral rules. Moral rules are commonly framed in terms of act species: Do not kill. Do not steal. Tell the truth. Keep your word. Rules of this kind sum up the rationale behind the classification of acts into species of the good and the bad (Brennan 1977:92). Much moral thinking then consists in classifying acts according to species types and invoking the relevant rule derived from moral education and custom to determine its basic character (that is, before matters of end and circumstance are taken into account). Moral rules can thus be distinguished from principles. It is essential to the use of moral rules that they relate in a clear way to species of act, whose presence or absence can be determined in the way Aquinas intimates. Their power to help in the guidance of action is lessened if they do not contain advice about which objectives/intentions to pursue. Principles, on the other hand, may deal in general or relatively abstract requirements upon action which do not directly rule in or out specific objectives. 'Respect autonomy' is a moral principle rather than a rule because it does tell us what specific intentions to pursue. It is a requirement that connects with our overarching ends in conduct, and through them indirectly with rules and specific acts. It would appear to be a requirement on a moral rule that what counts as obeying or disobeying it should be relatively easy to determine (though not whether its is *worth* obeying or disobeying). But no such requirement applies to moral principles for they set general ends in conduct.

More needs to be said about the nature of moral rules and their precise role in establishing the goodness and rightness of conduct. Enough has been done for the moment to illustrate the basis of a deontological approach to ethics: we have the nature of an act itself (determined by its objective) and we refer that to a moral rule to begin the task of establishing its moral status. We must now turn to the further definition of circumstances and motive.

The notion of the circumstances of an act is that of a range of relevant features which surround the act itself and enhance or detract from its moral merit. The distinction between 'act itself' and its 'surrounding features' can only be drawn if we have made use of something like the act's objective to provide boundaries which separate the act from what surrounds it. There are potentially a legion of things which the author of an act is or can be expected to be aware of which might add to or subtract from its worth. They include its time and place. Of particular importance for moral theory and the appraisal of action are those circumstances which effect its consequences. We can only distinguish an act from its consequences if, once again, we have a way of describing and delimiting an act's nature which does not take into account remoter features surrounding it. If the act's nature is determined by its objective then the result immediately aimed at in it is not a consequence, but any further, foreseeable results beyond that are. So, should I give money to the poor in circumstances where that entails impoverishing myself and bringing misery upon my dependants, then we have circumstances and consequences which bear decisively on the act's moral quality and which surround the character established by the objective alone. A human act is clearly not just a series of changes in the external world, but one can see the intuitive strength in the notion that its moral reality is decisively given through the multiplicity of its foreseeable effects in the world that surrounds it. This is the leading thought of consequentialist moral theories, to be explored further in the next chapter.

So far the delineation of the circumstances of an act appears straightforward, save that we need some principles of relevance to guide our choice of what features are to be included under the heading of its circumstances. But the difficulties in discovering such principles of relevance is highlighted by a point which Aquinas notes. Often what counts as a circumstance of an act in one case gets properly incorporated into the description of the act itself in another case. Place can be a morally relevant circumstance in considering acts of stealing. We might normally think that to steal from an orphanage is worse than stealing from a large department store. But when we consider stealing from a church, then we have not merely theft but sacrilege (Aquinas 1966a:41). According to Aquinas a feature such as place ceases to be a mere circumstance, but transforms the nature of the act (puts it into a new moral species) when that feature introduces a new species of evil (or good) into the act. Stealing from a church does this, because it entails breaking the special obligations of justice and respect owed to God. So it is not just a bad form of the act of theft. A clearer example might the relationship betwen the act of having sexual intercourse and the act of rape. In the latter case the circumstance of acting without the consent of the partner is present. This transforms the act from a morally neutral kind into one which embodies a specific form of evil. The feature is then not just another circumstance surrounding the act but is the prime determinant of its moral nature. Thus we think of the intention to have intercourse with another without consent as different in kind from the intention to have intercourse with another's consent.

The problem this phenomenon of the transforming circumstance creates is that of finding some non-arbitrary way of deciding when circumstances have this power of changing act descriptions and classifications. Aquinas writes vaguely of the discovery of a new conflict with reason being located in those circumstances that have this transforming power. But it is evident that the mere general thought of reason's demands is of no use in isolating cases when circumstance transforms objective. Only if we have specific standards which give us principles of likeness and difference between acts could we see that acts of rape were alike in being special offences against reasonableness in conduct, but unlike, in this respect, acts of intercourse performed with consent. Only a system of moral concepts with accompanying rationales for the classification of objectives and acts would establish these likenesses and unlikenesses and enable us to give thoughts about the reasonable and the unreasonable any content. We shall return at the end of this chapter to consideration of the significance and source of our act classifications.

So far have defined motive as the over-arching purpose or more general aim accompanying a specific intention/objective. The English word 'motive' covers a great variety of purposes and desires that can accompany actions. There are hints that Aquinas' notion of an end which I have connected with motive is meant to capture a particular kind of general purpose that can shape the pursuit of particular objectives. This sense is very important in the characterisation of aretaic moral theories.

Aquinas introduces the notion of the end of an act thus: 'The fourth [aspect of an act's worth] is according to its end, in other words, by its bearing on the ultimate cause of goodness' (1966a:19). Later on he states that the ultimate end of the human will is 'the supreme good' (77). When he cites giving alms in order to show off as a morally relevant end of action (87) he refers to something which is an instance of what we mean by motive. But he is, I think, particularly concerned with how the presence of such an accompanying end or motive would show the nature of the agent's conception of the good and how he or she stood in relation to the true human good. If desiring to show off is not just an incidental, passing aim of the actor, it may indicate his or her general life-aims. It could indicate that this person set great store by social advancement and prestige. It might point to a general goal of social recognition in the form of admiration and public status. Now whether we agree with aretaic moral theory or not, we can at least see some initial plausibility in the notion that an agent's ends or motives in the sense outlined are the ultimate determinant of the worth of his acts. What concentration upon ends (as defined) does is bid us to see particular acts with their objectives as part of a life plan and as embodying a vision of the good. It thus tells us that the worth of a particular action can only be finally settled in the light of its connections with the other acts the agent performs. When we consider performing an act ourselves, it bids us to consider how this act fits in to the living of a good life, whether its performance would embody and promote a pursuit of the good (whatever that might be). Such thoughts look as if they might be fit to serve as the basis for an over-arching means of ordering and grounding other ethical considerations. So when we say that aretaic theories concentrate on the motive of action as determining its worth, it is this special, uncommon sense of motive that is in view, namely the agent's ends and their relation to the good life.

WEIGHING THE QUALITIES OF AN ACT

The picture outlined so far enables us to describe a traditional view of the process of assessing the morality of conduct. This is a view implicit in much ordinary moral thought, relied upon in much traditional moral theology and espoused by Aquinas himself.

The most important feature of this traditional approach is the primacy it gives to objectives/intentions in determining the moral quality of an act. It relies on the idea that moral judgements are made for the most part by relating a set of moral rules (taught by custom, and backed by reason and / or revelation) to a range of act species. Act species are established, as we have seen, by reference to objectives/intentions. Such rules and act species give us an array of act types which are established as classes of obligatory, permitted or forbidden actions. The role of ends (motives) and circumstances (consequences) is fundamentally that of adding to or subtracting from the moral merit established by the matching of rules to species. There is room on this view for various sorts of moral exploration. We can debate the proper source and justification of moral rules. We can argue about the relative strength of rules. We can reflect in particular cases about which act species a performance fits into and which rules apply to it. We can ponder on whether the nature of the act's motive and circumstance are such as to take this instance of a moral species out of its classification as obligatory, permitted or forbidden and transfer it into another category. Though this picture of moral thought makes that thought rule-based, it does not inevitably make it legalistic in a pejorative sense of that term. For it can allow for kinds of flexibility about the classification of acts and the assessment of their worth.

Two consequences of this approach are worth noting. One is that it entails that a good motive is not sufficient for an act to become acceptable and right. This thought can also be expressed by saying that good intentions do not guarantee good action. 'Motive' and 'intention' in these dicta have none of the technical meanings we have given to them in the discussion so far. They are a way of referring to the general notion that the fact that an act is well-intentioned, that the agent does what he or she considers to be for the best, does not settle the moral quality of that act. That an agent acts for the best in his or her view may mitigate an act that was otherwise wrong, but it cannot settle the question of its goodness on this view, because acts fall into moral kinds in virtue of the objectives embodied in them. In other words it matters vitally what is done in the pursuit of what the agent considers to be for the best. What is done (as opposed to the agent's perception of his reasons for doing it) is something that is fixed objectively, that is independently of the agent's thoughts about what is for the best. Consider: almost by definition acts of euthanasia in medicine are well-intentioned – they will be performed because their authors consider them the best or only way of bringing about relief of suffering. That they are done for the best cannot settle their moral character, however, because it remains true that acts of euthanasia are acts of homicide, and any act of killing is one about which we must pause and ask specific questions to determine whether it was licit or not. If we consider an instance of euthanasia wrong, because it failed to be backed up by the reasons required of any justified killing, then its character as a well-intentioned act would not make it right. At most it might make us more lenient toward the author of the deed. It would not justify the act but it might shield its author from the reproach normally deserved by one who kills without justification.

The above point is captured well by Aquinas when he tells us that a good intention alone is not the whole cause of a good act of will (1966a:75). A leader may want to bring a just war to a successful and speedy end, but may not kill the innocent in order to do so. Aquinas extends this point by arguing that a good motive of this sort may not excuse even if the agent believed in conscience, sincerely but erroneously, that killing the innocent was a licit objective to enact in pursuit of the good end (1966a:65–7). For granted that the combination of act-species and moral rule tells us that this act is wrong, regardless of good intentions, the question arises of whether the agent *ought* to have known that it was wrong. It makes sense on the traditional view to state that the agent was in moral error. Some errors of opinion are culpable, as when we say that anyone who can believe *that* must be blind or perverse. The only explanation, short of madness, that we can give for leading Nazis believing in conscience that the Final Solution was required of them is by reference to defects of character that are gravely culpable.

Where the injunction 'Do those acts which are required by good motives' is interpreted in the non-techinical sense of 'Always act with good intentions, for the best' then it is obviously empty. It merely says 'Act as your conscience dictates'. No sincere action could then fail to match this principle. As indicated already and as will be explored below, aretaic moral theories have something much more precise in mind when they set out the idea that a good act is one that is embodies a good motive.

There is an important corollary of the traditional view of the moral importance of act species and the character of objectives which ties in with what has been said about the limitations of a morality of good intentions. This corollary is spelt out by Aquinas thus: 'some deeds are such that they cannot be well done whatever the good purpose or the good will' (1966a:89). This ties in with the Biblical injunction 'Do not do evil that good may come of it'. It is a way of affirming that a concern to produce the best consequences does not guarantee the rightness of an act. It matters, rather, what specific acts are done on the way to produce the best result. So, if the only means of producing a greatly beneficial result or of warding off a very evil consequence is the performance of an instance of a very evil act species (or, the violation of a particularly important moral rule), then the good result cannot be pursued in this way. This principle is vital in debates over the adequacy of consequentialism as a moral theory. Aquinas can espouse it because he holds that objectives/intentions can be morally assessed independently of motive and consequences and because he believes that assessment will give us a range of significant moral species, which will include a number of especially heinous moral types that may be forbidden regardless of when and how they are performed. This mode of reasoning does conflict with his teaching that one defect (such as one in the objective) makes an act evil. For that would make any act which was in violation of an objective-centred moral rule forbidden. The point of 'Do not do evil that good may come of it' is to pick out a specially evil class of acts which are forbidden regardless of circumstance, and so it must be part of an overall view which sees degrees of evil in moral species which may all be bad in some respect. In forbidding the performance of some species which are so evil, it implicitly permits the performance of others, which though bad may be licitly chosen in some circumstances. Many moral agents would accept that promise breaking and lying were inherently wrong, and yet agree that there are circumstances in which it is proper to achieve a good result or ward off a great evil by breaking a promise or telling a lie.

'Do not do evil that good may come of it' fits in ill with our common acceptance that promises are sometimes rightly broken and lies rightly told. It fits better with our thought that rape and murder are wrong no matter what their expected or actual results might be. We all might unreflectively agree that one may not rape or murder to bring about a great good or ward off a great evil. If we have this feeling, it will be connected with thoughts that the worthwhileness of an otherwise choiceworthy result of action is affected by the means we deliberately employ to bring about. With sufficient ingenuity we might imagine good results that might be achieved through rape or murder, but this might still leave us with a sense that such results would be sullied by the evil done to bring them about.

There are many philosophical problems in making the conceptual background behind 'Do not do evil that good may come of it' clear and acceptable to critical scrutiny. These problems will partly aired in this chapter and partly in the chapters on consequentialist and deontological moral theories. We have already noted that the principle depends on giving great weight to at least some moral rules that classify acts as evil, regardless of their circumstances and particularly their consequences. It follows that a consequentialist moral theory will have problems making sense of 'Do not do evil that good may come of it' and in granting it any authority. Consequentialist theories may accept that it is right to classify acts as good and bad by reference to their objectives alone, perhaps because as a rule of thumb we know that the vast majority of acts which have these objectives lead to worse results than any alternatives. Thus a rule 'Do not rape' might emerge as one with some utility. It may indeed gain authority within a consequentialist system as what Crombie calls a 'factitious' rule (Crombie 1966:250 and 258–9). The reason someone who rejects the notion of inherent wrongness may nonetheless accept factitious rules is that, though the rule in question has authority only as rough generalisation about which type of acts produce the best results, it may be better to hold such rules come what may. For if I allow myself to be tempted to set aside the rule easily I will produce worse results overall than if I resist this temptation. I can reach this conclusion if I compare the strength of the generalisation about worthwhile consequences behind the rule on the one hand, with the fallibility of any attempts to see if it can be set aside on the other. It is safer to act as if the rule is exceptionless. (The grounds of this kind of reasoning in consequentialism will be more fully explored in Chapter 4).

We need to search for other styles of moral reasoning to capture any sense that an act with an evil objective is inherently wrong or may sully the good results that can on occasion be achieved by performing it. Our discussions in Chapter 2 of the structure of moral relationships provides one way of doing this. Consider the convention and rule within the relationship of friendship that one should not deliberately deceive a friend. But on some occasions one might have to. Imagine that I have to deceive a friend, for the information that he wants from me will be used by him to injure another. Overall I act properly but I have done something which in part I regret. Regardless of other demands I have deceived one who had a special right to be treated honestly. To that extent the relationship has been damaged by violation of one of the key conventions that regulate and constitute it. My friend has been wronged and has a cause for complaint even though I acted properly overall. By the same reasoning, I might judge that if some scheme of mine to greatly benefit a friend could only be accomplished at the cost of gross deceit upon him, that scheme was sullied and improper regardless of how well it might turn out.

The principle that we should do not do evil that good may come of it depends on our being able to make the distinctions Aquinas draws between objective/intention and end/motive. In particular we must be able to distinguish between those results of an action that are pursued as its objective and those which are merely foreseen to flow from it. This shows us that the principle is intimately connected with another, namely the principle of double effect. The subsidiary principle of double effect is necessary to stop 'Do not do evil that good may come of it' producing a hopelessly narrow moral rigorism. The distinction between objective and foreseen consequences is needed in turn to enable double effect to perform this role.

The fact which threatens to overwhelm 'Do not do evil that good may come of it', and on which the principle of double effect bears, is that one act can have a multiplicity of effects. These multiple effects are often not of a uniform moral character. Good ones will be accompanied by bad ones. If 'Do not do evil that good may come of it' were interpreted as saying 'Never perform an act that has an evil effect' it would place restrictions on conduct of a kind that could not be tolerated. Consider an example from medical practice. A doctor may decide not to commence a new treatment on a terminally patient on the ground that this treatment is invasive and burdensome. He or she may do so in the reasonable certainty that an opportunity to extend this patient's days is thereby forgone. We may say then that one of the foreseen effects of the act is that the patient's death is hastened. While many people would regard such action as permissible, they might hesitate to do so if it were the case that the evil of hastening someone's death counted as part of the act's objective *in just the same way* as the effect of avoiding adding to the patient's burdens. We would not want to say that the effect of hastening death brought the principle of 'Do not do evil that good may come of it' into play at all. What the principle of double effect does is provide away of coping with the fact that acts have multiple, foreseen effects, by laying down that an act may be proper even though it brings about foreseen evil, provided that:

i.   The evil is not pursued as the objective of the act (either as an end in itself or as the means to an end).
ii.   The objective of the act is good.
iii.   The good in the objective is proportionate to the evil in the foreseen effects (that is, is sufficient to outweigh it).

Thus foreseen side effects of acts (effects that are not part of the act's objective) do not count in determining the moral species into which the act falls, and thus do not bring the act under the kind of moral rule that would make 'Do not do evil that good may come of it' relevant to its assessment.

Consequentialist moral philosophers typically attack the double effect doctrine, because they perceive it to be at the heart of defences of the non-consequentialist moral reasoning implicit in 'Do not do evil that good may come of it'. Many criticisms are offered, but the chief one relates to the cogency of the distinction between an act's objective and its foreseen side effects. Since this distinction is crucial to the entire scheme of traditional moral reasoning outlined in this chapter I shall briefly consider these criticisms here. (For a fuller treatment of this criticism and other questions relating to double effect see Byrne 1990.)

The difficulty of making a distinction between what an agent intends in an action and what he or she merely foresees arises out of the fact that what is said to be a side effect may be as certain as the result aimed at in the objective. (Consider: what I aim to do might not come off while I may know that my attempt will produce such and such accompanying results whether it succeeds or not.) So certainty cannot be a generally reliable guide in distinguishing objective from side effect. Moreover, not only must an evil side effect be foreseen in order to create the problem to which double effect is the answer, it must also be in some sense desired if double effect reasoning works. For if it is decided that foreseen evil can be brought about because tangential to the act and outweighed by a good objective, the agent must have decided that this evil is worth bringing about, all things considered. So he or she must both believe that the evil will result and desire, all things considered, to bring it about nonetheless. But many philosophers would regard belief and desire as sufficient for analysing 'intention'. What we intend to do is what we believe will result from our acts and what we desire to bring about. How then may side effect be distinguished from objective?

The distinction can be preserved if we add further conditions over and above belief and desire to our analysis of 'intention'. First we can note that a foreseen side effect is not aimed at in an act. If our doctor foregoes starting burdensome treatment and the side effect of hastened death does not materialise, he or she will not regard the act as abortive and its objective frustrated. The aim of not adding to the patient's burdens with this therapy has been accomplished. Second the agent is not endeavouring to bring the side effect about. If the side effect is not materialising, he or she will not take extra steps to ensure that it does. Though this effect is foreseen, the agent's actions do not track it and are thus not designed to ensure its realisation. Moreover, the bringing about of the side effect is not part of the agent's planning. The doctor will not be contemplating further acts of which the hastening of this patient's death is the precondition. It is incidental to his or her planning in this respect. So an objective of an act is an intended result of an act, not merely in being foreseen and desired in some sense. It is a result which in addition is aimed at, which the agent is endeavouring to bring about and which is an integral part of his or her planning as an author of action (see Bratman 1987:141–2).

The fact that effects pursued as part of an act's objective have these extra features indicate that they are closer to the agent's action than mere side effects and that they are of much greater relevance in determining its character as a member of a moral species. This point is reinforced when we consider that they also show that side effects are much less closely related to what Aquinas styles the end (or motive in our terms) of an act. An agent will typically pursue a particular objective as part of an overall search for the good as he or she sees it. Our doctor's objective in the case considered will be accompanied by overarching ends relating to the kind of good sought in the treatment of the terminally ill. Side effects –

not being intended, aimed, tracked or integral to planning – are marginal to the realisation of the good that figures in the act's end. Their relevance to the act's moral character is thus diminished, on Aquinas' analysis. The main purport of the principle of double effect is to determine the exact nature of the relevance of side effects. They must have some, for they are foreseen and figure in the agent's reasoning. But according to the principle they are not decisive in determining its moral character.

RULES AND MORAL REASONING

We have indicated in a preliminary way the kind of objections to the traditional view of moral reasoning that flow from consequentialism. More serious for this study are the objections from moral particularism, for these are closely connected with the limitations on moral theory and the importance of the particular case pressed in Chapter 2. Reflecting on moral particularism presents the possibility of revealing a deep inconsistency between the traditional view that moral reasoning depends, albeit only initially, on the application of rules to moral types, and the analysis of conscience offered in these pages. David McNaughton presents a case against the use of rules in moral reasoning and for moral particularism which can be reinforced by reference to Brennan's account of the nature of moral concepts (McNaughton 1988:190–205, Brennan 1977: Parts II and III). The essence of the case against thinking of the application of rules as being even the beginning of moral thinking that may be derived from McNaughton and Brennan can be set out as follows.

The kinds of acts mentioned in moral rules may either be moral kinds or not. If they are not, then there is no reason at all to suppose than they can be classed as either generally right or wrong. 'Telling falsehoods' picks out a class of acts which is not a moral kind. One can judge whether the truth has been told without making moral judgements. But whether telling a falsehood is morally justified or not is a matter that can only be settled by looking at an act of this type in a particular setting, that is along with its accompanying ends and circumstances. A rule such as 'Do not tell falsehoods' may be a useful rule of thumb to give to children before they are capable of making moral judgments and discerning moral likenesses and unlikenesses between acts. No intelligent moral agent, however, will approach the rights and wrongs of communication with this rule or think that rights and wrongs can be settled by appeal to such a rule. Whether a falsehood is rightly or wrongly told is a function of the entire set of morally relevant circumstances of a particular act. Since circumstances always alter cases, no one can hope to be alive to the morally relevant circumstances of a particular case by relying on a rule which picks out a type of act independent of its moral likeness and unlikeness to other acts.

The appearance that we can begin to make moral decisions through the application of rules may be explained as an illusion. We do have moral rules which deal in morally significant act species. Compare 'Do not lie' with 'Do not tell falsehoods'. Where the former is not just used as the equivalent of the latter, it picks out a class of acts which are morally alike: lying is the unjustified telling of falsehoods. Now we can settle matters of moral significance by deciding whether or not an act is an act of lying. But the decision is not reached through applying a rule to invariable and uncontroversial features of a situation. Whether this act is morally like other acts in being a lie takes moral discernment and vision to discover. These cannot be reduced to the application of rules and cannot be aided by concentrating, even initially, on only one feature of the case, namely the agent's objective.

The reason why the application of moral concepts cannot be explained in terms of the application of rules is that such concepts are open textured: there is no way in which what counts as a morally unjustified falsehood translates into a determinate and closed list of non-moral features of action (Brennan 1977:104ff). What we are guided by in deciding whether two acts are morally alike in being lies is not a list of non-moral features that we are sure all and only unjustified telling of falsehoods share. We are guided by the unspoken moral rationale behind this class of acts. And it may be argued that such moral rationales, which cannot be translated into rules dealing in non-moral kinds, are essential for judging whether acts are morally alike or unlike. For if we consider any one act defined by its objective, then there are myriad of facts surrounding it (facts about its author and its circumstances) that we might conceivably consider as relevant to its choiceworthiness. The end of our listing of factors we are aware of when we make a moral choice in a particular case will only come with fatigue and impatience. It is essential that we have some standards of relevance and these can only be moral standards, and we have seen that these cannot be expressed in terms of non-moral likenesses and unlikenesses. The cost of so doing is moral stupidity. Morally relevant features of action, picked out by the rationales behind moral concepts such as lying, cannot abstract objectives from the surrounding features of the agent's ends or the acts circumstances.

We have used some of the arguments of moral particularism in contending against both projectionist views of value and an over-reliance on moral theory. We are bound to concede something to this attack on the traditional view of moral reasoning. However, the attack is exaggerated in its claims and refuses to seek an accommodation between rule and particularism, even though one may be found.

In general we should avoid opposing respect for the particular case and reliance on rule. To adapt a remark of John Wisdom's quoted in Chapter 2: though in reasoning the final appeal is to cases, rules are of use in helping us bring one case to bear upon another. Respect for the uniqueness of the individual moral case should not blind us to see the need to understand it by reference to similarities and dissimilarities with other cases. In seeking an accommodation between moral particularism and the traditional view of moral reasoning two further points need to be borne in mind: first, that there is a continuity between moral and non-moral kinds; and second, that there is great utility in utilising objectives as the basis of moral kinds.

The importance of the first of these points can be brought out as follows. According to Brennan's account we must sharply distinguish these two interpretations of the rule 'Tell no lies': (a) 'Do not utter deliberate falsehoods' and (b) 'Do not utter morally unjustified falsehoods'. Rule (a) can be applied without taking in *all* the morally relevant features of an act, but it is morally insignificant. As (a) defines them, some lies are morally unjustified and some not. Moreover, (a) gives us no guidance on what the morally relevant features of an act of communication may be, since it contains no moral rationale. Rule (b) is a morally significant rule. It picks out acts as similar on account of a moral likeness they share. Its concept of lying will give us a moral rationale which helps us to pick out the relevant features of acts and their circumstances which make them lies (this will be a standard, by no means fixed, of what counts as a good reason for telling falsehoods). But the application of rule (b) in a particular case can only be decided by reference to the totality of relevant features of the act in question. Either way, the standard picture of moral reasoning based on moral rules that we find in Aquinas is mistaken.

The sharp distinction between moral and non-moral kinds in this argument is questionable, and seen to be so when the notion of lying is further examined. We may agree that the concept of lying in rule (a) is empty of moral significance and its rule of no particular value except as a rule of thumb. But we can have a morally rich notion of lying which at the same time is not equivalent to the simple notion of a morally unjustifed falsehood. 'Lying' is often used to refer to the uttering of falsehoods which amount to deceit. Deceit is a morally significant notion, but it is not equivalent to 'unjustified falsehood' and the question must remain open of whether some deceit is justified. Deceit is related to the moral notion of faithfulness in communication. If Auntie Flo, whose life-sustaining interest is the purchase and wearing of extravagant hats, asks her favourite nephew 'What do you think of this one; isn't it gorgeous', I do not lie if I say it is, even though I say that which I believe to be false. The question was not a request for information, but for reassurance. If I had responded to it with true information ('Its awful and a terrible waste of your money') it would not have been taken in, but rejected amid a flurry of consternation. The moral rationale in the notion of lying guides me in considering whether this act, in these relevant circumstances does or does not respect the demands of faithfulness in communication with another human being. Lies constitute a mode of disrespect for persons and are thus generally wrong. But I can sometimes rightly deceive, as when a violent and vengeful individual asks me where his intended, innocent victim is hiding. Here the demands of faithfulness in communication give way to those of avoiding harm to the innocent. Here Aquinas' model of weighing of objective in the light of end and circumstances fits. We are guided by moral rationales in deciding what surrounding circumstances are relevant: we in effect use two moral kinds: one from the objective (lying) and one from the end (safeguarding the innocent).

The continuity of moral and non-moral kinds can be brought out by reference to one of Brennan's own examples – murder (Brennan 1977:56–58). Brennan regards 'murder' as the label for killings that are wrongful, to be distinguished from homicides which are morally indifferentiated killings. This is somewhat simple. First, many folk use the notion of homicide in a morally significant way. Because of beliefs about the value of human life deeply embedded in our culture, most would assume that to describe an act as one of taking human life is at the same time to point out that it stands in need of strenuous justification. Homicides, we might say, have a tendency to be wrong unless justified. But murders are not just wrong homicides. They are homicides which cannot be justified by reference to certain standard reasons and considerations (see Devine 1978 for a full defence of this account of the meanings of 'murder' and 'homicide'). What is generally wrong with killing is that it is a violation of justice, of what is owing and due to persons, in this case one of the basic goods of personhood – life. Standard justifications of homicide, as in the case of the just war tradition or in defences of capital punishment, endeavour to present reasons why in justice another's life may be taken. That is, they will cite facts about the victim of intended homicide which might persuade us that he or she merits or deserves death or that death is somehow a good for this individual. Thus defences of medical killing (euthanasia) which stress the possibility that other duties to an individual could only be fulfilled if his or her life is brought to a painless end display the operation of this rationale. Whether such defences are accepted by all does not matter: even critics of euthanasia can recognise the intention behind such defences to take euthanasia out of the category of murder through appeal to facts about the victim and what is owing to him or her. Appealing to the benefits accruing to others through a person's death does not begin to take the act out of the category of murder. It follows from this that murder is not just wrongful killing. We can conceive of some killings which are not murderous though still wrong. They will be killings justified by reference to facts about the victim's deserts or good, but wrong because of the harm they would do to others. We can conceive of someone attempting to justify performance of an admitted murder. If a terrorist blackmails us by threatening the deaths of thousands unless we kill some innocent oppenents of his, and we thought it right to give in to such threats, we would have murdered for the sake of the good of others. Whether we would ever think such an act right does not matter, it is at least conceivable as an instance of a case of rightful killing that was also murder.

The above discussion illustrates that there are both genuine moral kinds which are not reducible to physical or natural ones and that there is no absolute gulf, but continuity, between moral and non-kinds. One final illustration of this point: consider the category of rape. All would agree that rape is a morally significant kind and the rule 'Do no rape' morally important. Yet 'rape' can be defined in natural terms: it is sexual intercourse performed without consent of the partner. Good reasons to do with the nature of sexuality, bodily integrity and respect for persons tell us that any acts so defined which we are ever likely to come across are impermissible. The moral rule forbidding rape is not just a rule of thumb, which has merely factitious validity. Circumstances might mitigate the personal guilt or wickedness of the rapist, but they won't tend to make us re-consider whether the act of rape is sometimes justified.

The second main point to be made against the particularist approach to moral rules consists in reminding ourselves once again of the value in seeking moral rules that fasten upon the objective of acts, without reference to motive and circumstance. Objective based act classifications give us moral species terms which can be applied without considering too much of the remoter consequences or surroundings of acts. They are thus of extreme utility in giving us initial classifications of acts which help us to focus our moral gaze. Such objective based classifications often use moral likenesses and differences between objectives, as I think the morally rich notion of lying I introduced above illustrates. Being morally rich such objective based classifications establish criteria of relevance which indicate what features that surround the objective might justify the performance of the act. But being objective based they do abstract from the total morally relevant set of features of a particular act. Thus they leave something under the headings of 'end' and 'circumstances' still to be considered. A rule such as 'Do not lie' (that is, tell a falsehood that amounts to deceit) is not then merely a rule of thumb. It does not merely sum up that we find more lies than not to be unjustified in the circumstances. It points to an inherent wrongness in lying. There is something in the objective of an act of lying that stands in need of justification and that may then be regretted even if justified. An act of lying embodies a mode of wrong relationship to another human being.

We must note an important consequence of using moral likenesses and differences between objectives for their description and classification. People with different moral standards and outlooks to my own will not necessarily share all the same act distinctions I make. Their moral world will in this respect be different from mine. The moral world of the religious believer who sees an important likeness between acts which are sacrilegious is different from that of the non-believer in this respect.

Two final points need to be made to bring this discussion of the nature of moral reasoning to a conclusion.

Brennan and McNaughton use their particularism to help defeat projectionist theories of value. If the kinds that figure in moral rules are moral ones, based on the perception of moral likeness and difference between acts, then we cannot say that moral notions are made up of a descriptive element plus a value element that originates in human attitudes. But if some morally significant kinds are also naturally explicable (as in the case of rape) then this enthusiasm to defeat projectionism must be tempered. Enough remains in Brennan's and McNaughton's point to question projectionist theories of value if a significant range of moral concepts remains irreducible to non-moral ones and if we remind ourselves of the need for principles of relevance in determining which features of action are to be considered when judging moral status. What emerges out of our discussion is a continuity in discontinuity between the realms of moral meaning and natural meaning in the human world. This is perhaps a better overall view of the relationship between the moral and the non-moral.

From our account there emerges not an out and out rejection of moral theory but a defence of a limited need for it. Rejection follows if moral rules are impossible except as *post hoc* summaries of the way moral investigation of particular cases has gone. If rules are allowed some life independent of their application in particular cases, then the need to introduce coherence into such rules by means of overarching principles and the need to ground those principles can be seen as legitimate. A *limited* only use for theory follows from the fact that much moral thought goes into the *application* of rules, since they frequently deal in kinds which are not reducible to non-moral categories. Such moral knowledge cannot be captured by rule or theory. It consists essentially in insight and analogical thinking which enable us to appreciate the individual case and its relationship with other cases. It can be conveyed by description and example and so is shareable and discussable. But in the end it is not captured by rule and principle.

4

Consequentialist
Moral Theory

THE CHARACTER OF CONSEQUENTIALISM

In the next three chapters we shall be examining the claims of the different forms of moral theory that emerge from moral philosophy. Consequentialist, deontological and aretaic moral theories each fasten on one of the facets of action that we normally take to be relevant to assessing its moral worth. One of the tasks moral theory might usefully accomplish is to set out in greater detail how each of these facets of action contributed to moral decision making and judgement. However, both consequentialist and deontological moral theories in our time have been offered as ways of simplifying and re-fashioning ordinary moral thought through the means of showing how their favoured dimensions of moral assessment somehow eliminate or ground the others. This is particularly true of consequentialist moral theory, which has aimed to show how forms of moral assessment other than weighing the worth of the results of action are at best provisional, or at worst reducible to consequentialist reasoning.

We shall approach consequentialist and deontological moral theories in this light: as attempts to reconstruct or reground moral thought on the basis of the exclusive role or priority of one facet of action and moral assessment. Seen in this way such theories are then bound up with the pretensions of moral philosophy itself. In offering a form of moral theory with these aims, philosophy can offer a definitive re-ordering and grounding of moral insight, replacing 'intuitive' judgement by theoretically sound deductions and calculations. We shall see in this respect a notable difference between representative consequentialist and deontological theories, on the one hand, and aretaic theories on the other. We shall discover that the last are typically built on quite a different picture of the relation between ordinary moral judgement and philosophical reflection and accordingly have quite different goals.

There are many versions of consequentialist moral theory, but if they are to achieve the aims described above they must share some common structural properties (compare Frey 1984a:4–5, Sumner 1987:171–3). They must posit some morally important good or goods which are clearly detectable as the results of action. If this good or goods are in the ultimate the sole source of moral worth and sole topic of moral assessment then they must have various features. First, their presence or absence must be detectable without reference to consideration of the motives or intrinsic nature of acts. Second, judging the absolute or relative worth of the goods resulting from acts must be possible by reference to the character of these goods alone, without reliance on other forms of putative moral judgement. This in turn suggests, third, that the morally relevant good or goods produced by conduct be numerically measurable, so that it is nothing other than the amount or quantity of good resulting from action that determines its rightness. Fourth this leads us to conclude that if the theory opts for one intrinsic good it must be strictly measurable across the various contexts of its occurrence; or if it posits a number of intrinsic goods, they must be strictly commensurable, so that their presence as the results of action gives us varying, comparable and quantifiable measures of a single overarching good. With a good resulting from action of this kind and the assertion that the amount of this good makes actions choiceworthy or not, the theory finally needs an appropriate mathematical function which determines what the optimal state of this good is. This function is typically that of seeking the maximum amount of good (though there are versions of consequentialism which offer different ways of determining the optimal state – so long as these are mathematically expressible the essence of the approach is not disturbed). For simplicity's sake 'maximising the good' will be taken in this chapter as the appropriate mathematical function of the good that consequentialism seeks.

These various ideas produce a simple core to consequentialist theories. There is a single intrinsic good (or if many intrinsic goods, they are all strictly commensurable). Actions are right if they promote the greatest quantity of this good. The hegemony consequentialism exercises over other forms of moral assessment now becomes clear. Morally important motives of action tend to collapse into one: the desire to promote the good as defined by the theory. Rules and the intrinsic nature of acts become at best of secondary importance. A rule such as 'Do not murder' tends to be treated as a rule of thumb, valid only because for the most part killing does not promote the intrinsic good, but the theory cannot allow the thought that an act type could have of itself intrinsic worth, be it negative or positive.

Frequently, though not inevitably, consequentialist moral theories are encountered as forms of utilitarianism. Utility is often cited as the ultimate good (or common measure of the worth of goods) sought as the result of action. In turn, utility has been associated through early expounders of utilitarianism (such as Jeremy Bentham and John Stuart Mill) with happiness. Happiness becomes the intrinsic good whose maximisation can be the standard of rightness. In the classical utilitarian tradition happiness has been thought of as a state of mind or consciousness: it is the presence of pleasurable sensation and the absence of painful sensation. So conceived it appears to have two advantages as an intrinsic good for a consequentialist theory. First it seems on the surface to be a separable, identifiable and quantifiable good produced by action. Second it apears to be true that most people accept that happiness as the presence of pleasure and the absence of pain is an intrinsic good (indeed it would be *prima facie* odd to assert that pleasure was not desirable) and there might be little shared agreement on other intrinsic goods. Therefore there is some chance that we can agree that it is the chief or sole intrinsic good. However, there is no agreement in the utilitarian tradition that happiness, so defined, is the appropriate measure of utility. Other versions of utilitarianism are: preference utilitarianism and welfare utilitarianism. The former defines utility as the satisfaction of preferences. It measures good by the number and strength of the preferences an action affects. Actions are right if they result in the best net satisfaction of preferences. Both classical and preference utilitarianism offer a subjective measure of utility, tied, respectively, to states of mind and the actual desires of individuals. Welfare utilitarianism offers an objective standard of utility in the promotion of welfare, where this consists of such things as life, liberty, health and the like. We shall concentrate on subjective versions of utilitarianism in this chapter, though some of the reasons behind, and issues raised by, objective, welfare accounts of utility will be touched upon. (Readers should consult Sumner 1987, chapters six and seven, for a full introduction to this species of utilitarianism).

If we concentrate on consequentialism as either classical or preference utilitarianism, it is a straightforward task to set out its advantages as a moral theory. These chiefly consist in simplicity and definiteness. Indeed, it is in virtue of appearing to display these two qualities so well that utilitarianism offers the best hope of fulfilling the maximum pretensions of moral theory, namely to show how all moral judgements worth defending can be deduced unproblematically from a general principle that has in turn been validated by philosophy. Utilitarianism offers to fulfill the pretensions of moral theory as a result of: abstraction on the source and nature of value and an offer of a quantitative means of measuring value. Its further perceived advantages stem from these two features.

In abstracting from all other alleged relevant moral values utilitarianism offers a simple, unproblematic account of the good. There is one, comprehensible good that is intrinsic. Other things are good only if they instrumentally promote this good. Even if it acknowledges that intrinsic good is manifested in different things (such as life, health, liberty) it teaches that these are commensurable and comparable. It follows that there are no irreconcilable values. If we are faced with a choice between two instances of the basic good (or two basic goods) we can simply be advised to choose the measurably greater one. Choices between instrumental goods resolve into calculations about their probable tendency to promote basic good and the amounts of basic good so promoted. It follows that moral thought, across all contexts and issues, can be expressed in terms of a common currency. These results of the abstraction and definiteness which utilitarianism introduces into moral thinking are linked with two tendencies of modern moral, social and political thought which utilitarianism undoubtedly promotes: an 'economic' and a secular approach to socio-political questions.

By an economic approach to social and political questions is meant one that seeks to solve them, not by appeal to established rights, privileges and customs, but by reference to the calculation of the overall outcome in costs and benefits of competing solutions. It is characteristic of reforming, democratic politics and social thought that they tackle social issues in this spirit. It is equally characteristic of modern forms of social decision making that they have little time for any appeal to the alleged deliverances of religion in providing answers to important questions. It is part of the dynamics of democratic politics and social thought that it should approach matters thus, seeking a common currency for dealing with issues and calculative methods of solving them. Utilitarian methods are obviously congenial to such ways thinking. Equally, utilitarianism has taken on the mantle of an obviously 'modern', that is scientific, secular and democratic way of approaching practical problems.

The secular character of utilitarianism is evident first in its account of the source of value: human pleasures and pains, or preferences are all that need exist for there to be morally relevant value in the world. Moreover no recourse need be had to faith or religious tradition in measuring the quantity of this morally relevant value. But though utilitarianism has been the tool of moral and social secularists, it must not be assumed that happiness or preference based forms of consequentialism are inevitably anti-religious or anti-theistic. While such forms of consequentialism do not *require* a religious basis for moral value and moral reasoning, they do not *exclude* it. Quite apart from a British eighteenth century theological tradition which interpreted divine commands for human conduct as prescriptions for the attainment of human happiness, we may cite the content of contemporary situation ethics as a form of Christian utilitarianism. In practice the situationalist's demand to follow only one moral principle, that is 'Do whatever love requires', can only be given any precise content if interpreted as the injunction to obey the dictates of benevolence on all occasions and above all else. The situationalist's down-playing of moral rules and preaching of the demands of *agape* comes down to a form of happiness maximisation (see the quotations and references in Fairweather and McDonald 1984:56ff for proof of this).

It is plain that utilitarianism has much to recommend it as an account of the foundations of ethics where the pretensions of moral theory are taken seriously and where the claims of rival theories, such as deontology are rejected. But is there anything like a proof that utilitarianism must be the correct account of morals? Proof in this context might come from at least two sources: either from showing that the theory is the only one that makes sense of our ordinary moral judgements or from an argument to the effect that the essence of morality entails the truth of the theory. The former method of justification is unlikely to be persuasive, for reasons which if they are not clear now will become so later in this chapter. There are two arguments of the second type that are worth considering. Both begin from the universal nature of moral judgement and conclude that only utilitarianism captures this properly.

The first of these arguments can be constructed out of some remarks in L. W. Sumner's *Abortion and Moral Theory* (1981, Sumner only uses the argument negatively – to exclude a religious foundation for morals). It depends on the premise that:

> . . . any facts marshalled in favour of a particular [moral] view must be publicly accessible. Since science is our established procedure for confirming or disconfirming beliefs about the world, factual claims must be subject to some form of empirical verification. (Sumner 1981:38)

From this thought some conclude that only a utilitarian reconstruction of moral thought allows it to be based upon publicly accessible, because empirically verifiable, grounds and reasons. Since it is part of the essence of moral judgement that it and its grounds be publicly accessible, the case for utilitarian consequentialism as the only possible rational reconstruction of morality is strong – provided the premise that scientific reasoning is the paradigm of publicly checkable argument is accepted. It is in this spirit that utilitarian writers will refer to alternatives to consequentialist reasoning as 'superstitious' (compare the tone of the defence of utilitarianism in Smart 1973; we shall return to the argument that religious ethics is inevitably superstitious and irrational in Chapter 8).

Non-utilitarians will turn the force of this argument by maintaining that there are other forms of publicly shareable reasoning and insight outside of those demonstrated in natural science. To suppose otherwise can justly be represented as a false 'scientism', in the end harmful to a true respect for science because leading to a false application of its methods to areas where they may come into disrepute. In the earlier chapters of this study I tried to illustrate, from the work of John Wisdom and others, the point that reasoning in the humane studies may be universal in intent and publicly shareable, yet display a logic that is distinctive. Until all such efforts to develop alternative paradigms of reasoning for ethics have been shown to be futile the argument for utilitarianism under consideration remains at best a challenge to alternative accounts of moral thought – to show how on their view there can be proper public argument on moral issues which has some prospect of reaching agreement and claiming universal assent. The argument will also alert the critic of utilitarianism to a weak point in consequentialist ethics, namely the admission (to be discussed below) from within consequentialism that its methods of moral demonstration cannot always be used directly to calculate the rightness and wrongness of acts. This inevitable tendency to fall back on non-consequentialist reasoning as at least a temporary substitute must soften any contrast between utilitarian science and non-utitilitarian superstition.

Such a contrast between utilitarian and non-utilitarian moral judgements is implicit in R. M. Hare's argument for the necessity of a utilitarian outlook. Hare employs a distinction between critical and intuitive moral judgement. The latter is the raw material on which moral reflection sets to work, but it has no intrinsic claim to certainty or knowledge. Intuition is embodied in our first-hand, immediate decisions about how to act. Since such decisions often lead to conflicting judgements, both within a single agent's thinking and between the thought of different agents, we need a way of sorting out which moral intuitions are reliable or have priority and which not. We then move to the critical level of thought which must be different in kind: 'at that level no appeals to intuition are allowed, because the function of critical thinking is to judge the acceptability of intuitions, and therefore it cannot without circularity invoke intuitions as premises' (Hare 1981:131). To provide a method for critical moral thought that does not side with any pre-given moral intuitions we need to appeal to morally neutral facts and to principles derived from the undisputed 'logic' of moral terms. Hare's argument is then that from such facts and the logic of moral terms such as 'ought' we can deduce that a form of preference utilitarianism is the only possible form of critical moral thinking.

Hare's deduction of preference utilitarianism depends on his thesis that moral judgements are universalisable (as discussed in Chapter 1 above). If I face a moral situation in which two of my hitherto reliable intuitions conflict, any resolution of them in the form of a judgement 'I ought to do so-and-so' contains no essential reference to me and my preferences. If valid it holds for anyone similarly circumstanced. Thus I must think that my judgement in resolution of the conflict of intuition would be valid and commendable to all those persons involved in the situation in question and potentially affected by the practical policy I lay down in my critical moral judgement. But 'acceptable and commendable' to them can only mean 'acceptable in the light of all their preferences'. I must put myself in their shoes and produce a policy which represents a fair resolution of their individual interests. This entails that my critical policy must maximise as many of the interests (that is, preferences) of the parties affected and involved. But this is to reach a preference-utilitarian solution to the practical problem. As the preference utilitarian sees it, justifiable practical decisions affecting, actually or potentially, many people are like rational decisions made for one individual: one itemises the various preferences relevant to the decision (whatever they are and whoever has them: they are relevant simply in virtue of being capable of being affected by whatever decision is made and acted upon). Then one adopts that policy which maximally satisfies the preferences concerned, where maximal satisfaction is a function of the number and strength of the preferences affected (compare Hare 1981:42–3).

We saw in Chapter 1 that it is a moot point whether universalisability is function a distinct meaning of words used in moral contexts or a substantive demand for impartiality which is part of the customary essence of moral thought. Though a verdict against Hare on this point would affect the status of his argument it would still leave it with some force. Suppose, as I have contended, that universalisability (the view that moral judgements make no essential reference to specific persons, times and places) is a substantive demand upon a moral outlook and not a truth of meaning. It still follows that any moral view with any prospect of being commendable to others will have to embody *some* form of impartiality and universalisability. Hare's claim is then that the only defensible form of impartiality, and the one that is current in ordinary moral judgement, is the kind enshrined in preference utilitarianism. Impartiality is best and usually interpreted (albeit tacitly) as maximally satisfying the extant preferences of all those affected by a moral policy. Is this true?

Whether Hare's interpretation of impartiality in moral judgement at all accords with its ordinary understanding can brought into serious question by considering an example. I find myself in one of Hare's 'conflict situations'. I have hitherto relied on both the moral intuition 'It is right to further a friend's interests' and 'It is wrong to sexually abuse children'. Now I discover that one of my close friends indulges in child rape and seeks my aid in furthering his projects of pleasure. Now on Hare's view the resolving, critical judgement against child rape and against offering the aid of friendship to further it can only be universalisable if taking all relevant interests (that is preferences) into account I see that this would maximally satisfy the set. But this would mean taking into account my friend's preferences for raping children and seeing that they had been properly weighed in the balance against those of others affected by his preferences. Most folk, not antecedently convinced of the truth of preference utilitarianism, would regard this as absurd. Just because they were preferences for something evil they had no weight in deciding what is impartially right.

But if I give my 'intuition' that child rape is wrong initial weight against my friend's view that it is an acceptable form of pleasure, is not my resolving, critical judgement reached partially? How can it claim impartiality? These questions would have force if the only way of seeing our respective preferences (for and against child rape) was as nothing other than that: bare preferences with nothing more to be said in favour of one or the other. But such a view of their status reflects a further, substantive philosophical opinion, namely that there are no independent values against which the worth of preferences can be tested. Given that position it may be that impartiality in moral judgement can only be interpreted along Hare's lines. By the same token another obvious interpretation of impartiality is ruled out. Moral judgements may be impartial and universalisable because they embody thought about agent-neutral goods, that is values which obtain or otherwise independent of the preferences of individuals (Sumner 1987:169–170). On this understanding of the goods relevant to action my thought that child rape is wrong and thats its wrongness outweighs the claims of friendship is critical, impartial and universalisable if it represents genuine reflection on the objective harm of child rape, the objective disvalue of friendship pursued for ignoble ends and between those not united in respect for the virtues, and so forth. I can commend my judgement to others not because I think it will maximise preferences in the fashion of Hare but because I think it a defensible account of what is good and worthwhile to pursue independent of all preferences. I think, if my judgement properly embodies the form of morality, that my judgement draws upon reasons for action which are independent of my personal preferences because they reflect the preference-independent value (negative or positive) of actions and states of affairs.

Hare's deduction of utilitarianism is seen to have strong internal consistency. Given a preference dependent view of value, the distinction between intuitive and critical thought follows neatly, as does the negligible status of 'intuitive' moral judgements. With equal neatness it follows that the only escape from personal preference into objectivity (in the form of: impartial, universally commendable judgement) must be a technique of isolating, appreciating and aggregating all preferences affected by moral decisions. But none of these moves are based upon truths of definition. Rather they rest on substantive interpretations of how moral judgement can be grounded and should proceed. The non-preference-utilitarian thinker will give different, substantive interpretations of impartiality and related notions. If mistaken, he is not guilty of error about a theory-neutral meaning or logic to moral discourse. Preference-utilitarianism, if correct, is not so because it can be deduced from truths of meaning. It looks as if Hare will have to provide a different kind of justification for his theory, which, like others, will have to make some appeal to congruence with our pre-theoretical understanding of morals, which perhaps means giving that understanding greater weight than Hare's intuitive/critical distinction allows.

The question of the congruence between utilitarian thought and ordinary moral judgement is one that raises itself when criticisms of utilitarianism are discussed. For we have seen that there is little reason to suspect that there is a strict proof of utilitarianism. Criticism of utilitarianism is best considered under two heads: accounts of the basic good and of the consequentialist method.

THE BASIC GOOD

Criticisms of the basic good postulated by classical and preference versions of utilitarianism can be both internal and external. Internal criticisms will concentrate on whether the basic goods selected meet the demands of the theory. External criticisms will query whether on independent grounds pleasure or preference satisfaction are intrinsic goods capable of being the foundation of all value.

The internal demands of utilitarian theory entail that a basic good such as happiness, thought of as the presence of pleasure and the absence of pain, should be a measurable quality, identifiable and assessible independently of the activities and states of affairs that it accompanies. These demands committed Bentham and his followers to a particular view of pleasure: it had to be thought of as a mental state detachable from human activity. Only in this way might I think that I could compare the happiness to be gained from writing a philosophy book in my study with lazing in the afternoon sun in my garden *without* reflecting on the worth of these respective activities in relation to my values and interests. If we start to think of the range of things we find enjoyment and satisfaction in it becomes hard to think that the pleasure we take in them consists in their being accompanied by different degrees of an isolatable and homogenous mental state, as it were a kind of inner 'tingling' that is brought on by doing them. If I ask myself why I find writing philosophy books pleasurable or more pleasurable than other things, I am asking why I find this activity satisfying, rewarding and so forth. And such questions relate to the point and worth of the activity as much as (or more than) they do to its psychological accompaniments.

There appears every reason to diagnose an old fallacy behind the view of pleasure (and thus happiness) in classical utilitarianism: because we use the one noun in talking of the pleasure we find in poetry, ice-cream, music, horse-riding and a million and one other things, so some assume that there is one, homogenous substance that it names. What is wrong with the classical view is not that we do not judge of the worth of things without some reference to the pleasure to be found in them, nor that we cannot compare the pleasures of different activities. The mistake lies in the picture presented of the nature of these judgements, and in particular the assumption that that they can be made using quantitative means and without reference to independent forms of value.

Preference utilitarians have thought that counting and measuring people's preferences for activities and states of affairs provide an alternative way of making a utilitarian calculus internally consistent. It is certainly true that for certain purposes, perfected by economists in particular, it is possible to establish the range and comparative strength of the preferences relevant to a practical choice and thus provide determinate measures of the utility of possible ways of making the choice. For certain limited practical questions, such as the design of buildings or the manufacture and pricing of consumer goods, we may be able to delimit the range of people affected by the possible outcomes of choice, and identify which preferences these people have which are relevant and how strong they are. Critics will question how far this is possible in judging important moral and social questions. However, they are more likely to stress in this context the apparent oddity of making preference in general a source of value. Surely, it will be argued, it is wrong headed to make people's preferences the indicator of the value they find in things, for people have a preference for something because they think it valuable, and not the other way around. (Compare: people do not find statements to be true because they believe them; they believe them because they judge them to be true.) In which case in determining how to resolve moral and social questions we should be looking at the *reasons* for people's judgements of value and not at the preferences that result from those judgements.

This last point takes us on to external criticisms of utilitarianism's account of the basic good, to which we shall now turn.

Classical utilitarianism's account of the basic good shows it to be a derivative from hedonism and it is subject to many of the criticisms of levelled at hedonism as a portrayal of intrinsic and basic value. If pleasure is a separable and measurable state of mind why should anyone suppose that its realisation is the most important goal of conduct? It appears to be a totally impoverished view of the human good to suppose that the maximisation of such a state of mind is the ultimate good. This is so not least because some of the ways in which we find and can imagine pleasure being realised devalue it utterly. Thus some people gain pleasure through the use of narcotic and mind-numbing drugs. It hardly seems right to say that the reason why this is wrong is that they thereby forego other, later pleasures for themselves or diminish the happiness of others. In Aldous Huxley's *Brave New World* the use of narcotic, pleasure inducing drugs ('soma') has been so perfected as to eliminate personal side-effects and social distress, on the contrary 'soma' intoxication works as a means of spreading personal and social pleasure. It is wrong nonetheless because it is a demeaning way to live. Does utilitarianism have any room for this thought? These thoughts about the poor guide that pleasurable experience offers to the presence of value can be strengthened through the reflection that pleasurable experience is compatible with delusion and the abandonment of all normal human activity. As a refinement to narcotic intoxication consider Robert Nozick's idea of the pleasure machine (developed and discussed in Finnis 1983:36ff). This is an imagined sources of messages to the brain, capable of giving it all the experiences of reality while the subject sits back and does nothing but put in the programme. Here we can envisage someone gaining all the experiences involved in partaking in worthwhile activities, though in reality nothing is achieved or participated in. That this would hardly appear to be a good, far from it, indicates the strength of our thought that pleasure is worthwhile as an aspect of the worthwhileness of the activities and states of affairs it accompanies and not as an independent source of value.

Because utility is seen as the intrinsic good which is the source of all value so the utilitarian is forced to rely on the actual direction of people's pleasures as the measure of value, rather than the pleasures they ought to have. This is bound to produce results which make utilitarianism seem unattractive to anyone not antecedently convinced of its intellectual necessity. For example, the utilitarian would have to allow a case to be made for the moral acceptability of slavery in a society with widespread ownership of slaves based upon the damage to the pleasures of owners from abolition. Though the utilities are probably most unlikely to balance out in favour of slavery in an actual case, it could theoretically be made and could not be dismissed on the ground that the enjoyment of slave owning and its consequences was of no moral account or inherently wrong. Generally the classical utilitarian will have to admit that the pleasures evil people gain from doing vicious things are of positive moral importance. Though from any moral point of view child rape is wrong, it is better from a utilitarian point of view that, given the practice exists, child rapists should get pleasure from it (compare Brown 1986:31). Thus the amount of negative utility created by the practice is reduced, even though it still exists. I hazard that most people would view taking relish in such an act as worse than not enjoying it and would certainly be puzzled by the injunction to weigh the rapist's pleasures in the balance before forbidding his activities. Here, we have once more reflections which derive from the weaknesses in beginning from hedonism as an account of fundamental value.

It is clear that similar, external criticisms can be given of preferences and their satisfaction as the foundational source of value. Because preference satisfaction figures so largely in contemporary deontological theories we shall consider such criticisms more fully in the next chapter. For now we can point to the *prima facie* oddity in saying that satisfying preferences is the basic form of value. A person's preferences can be satisfied, that is fulfilled, without thereby satisfying him or her if they are preferences for the wrong things. From our discussion of Hare it seems counter intuitive to separate the value of a preference from the question of what it is a preference for. If preference satisfaction is intrinsically good, regardless of the content of preference, we will be forced to say that the murderer's or torturer's satisfied preferences at least provide *some* intrinsic good to outweigh the harm they do to their victims. Classical and preference utilitarianism seek a single, detachable and homogenous good that can serve as a basic value for utilitarian calculation. It is no doubt because their respective basic goods must have these features that they appear impoverished from an external point of view. Enriched accounts of a putative basic good will surely have to recognize that goodness is plural in its manifestation and cannot be detached from activities and modes of life. Some recent forms of utilitarianism accept the criticisms made of classical and preference versions and move toward seeing utility as residing in separate forms of human well being such as liberty, health, personal achievement and the like. The problem for an enriched account of utility of this sort is that its very richness promises to prevent it from being capable of fulfilling the formal demands of utilitarian calculation. Granted that personal states such as those listed can all be seen as facets of welfare or well-being, can they be quantified and can their relative quantities and values be established without reference to distinctively moral considerations? Though the reformed utilitarian might try to locate utility in separate activities and personal states he or she must still suppose that there is a common measure of utility, of the value of these states, and that questions of value of all kinds can be answered through a clearly mathematical operation on the measures of these components of utility. Authors such as Sumner and Griffin (Sumner 1987 ch. 6 and Griffin 1986 *passim*) have suggested that welfare or well-being is just such a common measure which is capable of supporting strictly consequentialist reasoning. The jury is still out on this line of argument.

CALCULATING THE RIGHT

In this section we shall be concerned with objections to utiltarianism that turn around the method of estimating the rightness of actions through calculation of their net beneficial and harmful consequences. Our discussion will begin by looking at alleged ways in which this method produces moral verdicts substantially at variance with ordinary moral judgement and will then explore whether utilitarian defences against this charge leave the consequentialist system internally consistent and adequate.

It is not difficult to find examples in the literature of putatve moral problems that would be dealt with one way by a consequentialist ethics and another way by the normal reflective conscience. Most of these examples are meant, by critics, to show that utilitarianism can pay scant regard to the central moral value of justice. One example, taken from an essay by van den Beld on medical ethics, suffices to illustrate this strategy of criticism (van den Beld 1988:93–94). Suppose doctors in a hospital have five patients, each in need of a different organ for a life-saving transplant operation. They also have a healthy, about-to-be discharged patient whose separate organs happen to be ideally suited for transplant into these five, dying individuals. Would it not be right, because productive of the greatest net good, to kill the reluctant donor in order to save the others? Now this is one case where ordinary morality would say 'Do not do evil that good may come of it'. The evil involved in this course of conduct might appear to be that of grossly violating what is due to one individual in order to benefit others. What is violated is the virtue and principles of justice. These bid us to give to each person his or her due. They bid us as part of this to take account of what an individual is or has done in deciding what is appropriate in the way of action which effects him or her. So that if someone is to be killed, justice, which looks backwards as much as forwards, asks what this person has done or is, in the way of character and disposition, so as to deserve death. It requires that we justify so treating this person by relevant facts about him or her, facts which indicate why this individual deserves death or why death would be in his or her interests. Now the very essence of consequentialist reasoning would appear to entail turning our backs on this entire mode of thinking. Such reasoning is entirely forward looking. What is done to a moral subject by way of harm can only be represented to reason as a given quantum of gross evil. If in specific circumstances net good for all those effected by the various possible courses of action available in these circumstances could be achieved by inflicting such harm, then the method of consequentialism bids us set aside justice as of no account.

Thus it can be argued that there is a fundamental clash between ordinary moral judgement and utilitarianism over the values inherent in justice. Justice, the critic will say, exists in part to constrain the pursuit of greatest future good, so cannot be accounted for on a utilitarian scheme. Rights can also be argued to play a similar role in our ordinary moral thought and so they too provide an area where utilitarianism fails to capture moral reality as we see it. Indeed important moral rights can be interpreted as claims people have which correspond to the duties owed to them in justice by others. Rights talk may be seen as a way of talking about the demands of justice from the point of view of those who are beneficiaries of the demands of justice (Finnis 1980:204–5). Our victim's right to life is not to be bargained against the good to others of killing him.

Awareness of the alleged clash between utilitarianism and ordinary morality on the score of justice is as old as utilitarianism. I shall take a very narrow path through the vast literature that has accumulated on this topic and deal only in the broad strategic questions which the issue raises.

A utilitarian reply to the justice objection has first to decide whether utilitarian theory is or is not going to be morally conservative. It is open to the consequentialist to argue from the basic premises of the theory that much of the content of the ordinary conscience is hopelessly muddled and in need of scientific restructuring. Fundamental clashes of the kind van den Beld's example is meant to illustrate are then discounted in advance by the intentions behind the theory. What presenting utilitarian theory as radically reformist does then is to rule out any defence of it as the theory which gives the best account of the workings of the ordinary conscience (those workings are not *worth* defending on this approach). Many contemporary utilitarians do not take this reformist line because they do not wish to rule out defending utilitarianism on these grounds. They therefore must adopt the strategic decision of arguing that such clashes between utility and justice are more apparent than real. It is only where some unstructured moral thought finds itself already wishing to cast aside some of the traditional restraints on rules about killing and the like, that they might wish to offer utilitarianism as an aid in a reformation of thinking already underway. Examples where such application of utilitarian thinking might be made would be found in medical ethics and particularly in the instances of euthanasia and withholding neonatal care.

Granted that the utitilitarian's basic approach will be to argue for a congruence of view between unrestructured conscience and the theory, we can explore the variety of options of maintaining this congruence.

One option consists of rule utilitarianism. This version of the theory states that calculations of utility are never legitimately applied to the rightness of particular acts. They are only applied correctly to moral rules. Individual actions are right or wrong by virtue of being prescribed or proscribed by an appropriate rule. Rules are judged to be correct on utilitarian grounds, by determining whether a general human practice corresponding to them would promote greater net utility than any alternative general practice. Now we can all think of reasons why a general practice of not deliberately killing innocent hospital patients was better than alternative murderous practices. The fact that a particular act of killing might promote greater net utility than alternative acts is irrelevant. The problem of the unjust act which promotes utility then dissolves. The act is wrong in the light of an established moral rule. We are forbidden by the method of rule utilitarianism to even raise the question of whether a specific violation of the rule would produce the best net consequences overall.

Most critics and defenders of utilitarianism now agree that pure rule utilitarianism will not work. It is neither consistent with the fundamental assumptions of a utilitarian outlook nor internally adequate. It cannot be the former if value for the utilitarian is fundamentally net utility. Given that, it is irrational to place a bar in principle on using this measure to determine the value of a specific act. It would be grossly irrational to perform an act to which there was a specific alternative known to have greater utility. Internal inadequacy of rule utilitarianism is shown by asking how specific are the rules which must be compared for their utility. Rules can be more or less detailed in the classes of action they prescribe or proscribe. No doubt if we consider the killing of our unwitting organ donor under the heading of a very general rule licensing homicides then, the rule being of dubious utility, the act will appear wrong on a rule utilitarian view. But let us consider it as licensed by a very specific rule on permissible killings, which would only allow a practice of killing in rare and detailed circumstances. Such a rule and practice might then promote greater utilty than alternatives and thus make the act right. Indeed it looks as if what a utilitarian must go for is a rule on homicides which states that killings are impermissible except where they individually yield greater utility than non-killings. Thus we can kill for the sake of utility without violating *any* worthwhile moral rule. So rule utilitarianism, if it thinks about what rules are the right ones to bring to bear on conduct, becomes equivalent to act utilitarianism. (See Smart 1973:10–12 for an elegant summary of these criticisms.)

The conservative utilitarian must take an alternative tack. It is not hard for him or her to argue that the embeddedness of actual and likely human acts in surrounding circumstances, including human expectations, is bound to mean that the knock on effects of departures from justice are such as to entail net losses in utility. Thus in our example, we can realise that once the doctors' act of killing became public admissions and referrals would fall off somewhat to say the least. The worthwhile utilitarian goal of healing the sick would thus be visibly frustrated. Potential volunteer organ donors would make themselves scarce and the short cut to improving the lot of those needing transplant would turn out to be a cul de sac.

The defence just offered aims to secure the key advantage of rule utilitarianism, namely that we can rely on normal rules of justice and the like, without its embarrassing attempt to shield decisions about particular acts from calculations of utility. Now the debate between critic and defender of utilitarian tends to fasten on whether there are in fact any plausible circumstances in which acts which would be forbidden by rules of justice would be approved by consideration of the utilities of acts possible in those circumstances. On the one hand the critic will try to present instances where the connections which give flagrant violations of justice or rights spin offs in negative utility are absent. Secret judicial killings of the innocent or hidden murders of unwanted orphans form the stock in trade of his arguments. The defender of utilitarianism will endeavour to show that such imagined cases are flawed, having some aspect or other that mitigates or removes the clash between utility and moral opinion. It is not a debate which has lead to much enlightenment and it is not clear whether the critic's strategy is at all helpful. From R. M. Hare's *Moral Thinking* we can develop a powerful argument which suggests that the strategy can never serve to rebut utilitarianism.

There is an inherent tendency for the examples of pure injustice (or rights violations) which have no utilitarian spin offs to be fantastic and far removed from anything likely to be found in real life. For the critic tries to construct examples of such wrong doing in which wicked actions lose their connections with the other acts, practices and institutions in which they are embedded. Policies of torture which are never to be detected and to have no implications for the respect attaching to, and the efficacy of, the administration of justice are going to be hard to come across. So it matters not that the critic can come up with acts in fantastic circumstances which conscience untutored by consequentialism would condemn. To succeed as a theory utilitarianism need only claim that the moral judgements we make in the real world are best justified by utilitarianism's favoured considerations. If in the real world utility gives the best account of why justice is good and injustice an evil, then that is all the theory and its critics can hope for. It can be of no bearing on its success as a moral theory in our world that it would yield judgements we might reject in a fantasy, make-believe world we shall never find ourselves in.

This counter from the utilitarian can lead us to refine our conception of what possible divergences between the deliverances of conscience and the theory may show. It may be correct that the very refinement of the examples used to point up the fact of divergence tends strongly to deprive the fact of divergence of falsifying power. However, it may be that the real force of such examples lies elsewhere: in showing that there are grounds of judgement and species of wrongness somehow central to our moral outlook but unintelligible to utilitarianism. The real wrong of murder for ordinary thought may be alleged to lie, not in its side effects for net, future utility, but in the wrong done to the victim, in the violation of what is owing to him or her and to the relationship which should obtain between us and that victim. Surely it is correct to test this 'intuition' by imagining a killing in which the side effects for future utility are absent and seeing if we would still say it is wrong, because unjust or a violation of the right to life. This indicates, not that utilitarianism is not to be trusted because it would give wrong judgements about the rightness of acts of killing, but that there is a mode of wrongness in admitted wrongful killing to which utilitarianism is blind. It therefore cannot come close to a proper account of the operations of conscience on important matters such as this.

The last point raises a critical issue for utilitarianism: even if it can produce answers to moral questions which match those of ordinary moral judgement, can it reproduce the content of traditional conscience? Can it, for example, explain why it is important to think in terms of merit, desert and what is owing to individuals? Conservative minded utilitarians think that these questions can be answered in the affirmative. They contend that though utilitarian calculation gives the right answer to practical questions for the right reasons, it does not follow that utilitarian reasoning is the best reasoning to use by ordinary moral agents in thinking about right and wrong. So both the content and decisions of a traditional conscience can be maintained.

What the utilitarian may appeal to are the alleged utilitarian advantages of encouraging ordinary moral agents to rely for the most part on non-consequentialist thinking in moral choice. The factors which make such a strategy reasonable include the following: inevitable ignorance about many of the long-term consequences of decisions; self-deception and bias in calculating that present evils can be outweighed by future goods (compare Hare 1981:147). Because of imperfect information gathering and processing (Sumner 1987:187) the utilitarian can be fairly confident that it is best to pursue the utilitarian good by an indirect strategy. This strategy will encourage people for the most part to think in non-utilitarian ways about right and wrong, and thus in terms of notions such as desert, merit, rights and the like, which are not primarily or mainly directed toward the maximising of good in the future. Thus the utilitarian introduces a distinction bewtween the theory as a method of decision and as a method of justification (Sumner 1987:178–9). For a variety of reasons, the traditional conscience with its non-consequentialist picture of the sources of right and wrong may be a good method for making moral decisions and utilitarianism does not therefore preach that the notions which provide its content should be abandoned. The value of utilitarianism emerges at two levels. In the first place, it provides an overall justification of the traditional conscience: acting and choosing on the basis of ideas of justice, rights and the like can be seen to promote utility in the long run. Second, as the appropriate theory of justification for moral judgements, utilitarian reasoning can be appealed to where principles and rules of a traditional kind lead to conflicts of duties or rights. It can also be used to cope with novel moral problems which find no ready answer in terms of traditional categories.

Indirect utilitarianism of the kind outlined is enshrined in Hare's distinction between intuitive and critical moral thinking. Utilitarianism provides the correct theory at the critical level which justifies our intuitive moral judgements and our reliance upon them. Where intuitions conflict critical thinking can be brought to bear directly on moral decisions, but for the most part there are good, critical reasons for thinking intuitively.

Indirect utilitarianism represents the most sophisticated attempt to cope with the implausibility of utilitarian thinking as judged by the standards of a traditional conscience. It will also be seen that it provides the resources for coping with other standard criticisms of the theory. For example it can be used to rebut the point that, in being visibly willing to trade off present evil for future good, the utilitarian encourages moral blackmail and the consequent debasement of moral and political life (compare Williams 1972:110–11). The question we must now pose is 'Does utilitarianism provide an adequate level of justification or critical thinking on which ordinary moral thought rests and in the light of which it may be developed and improved?' This question must be answered in the negative if utilitarianism has no proper conception of the basic good, as suggested above. Further discussion must focus on two issues: how much of traditional conscience is preserved and how far utilitarian reasoning can really support it.

Though indirect utilitarianism can aim at leaving traditional moral categories and judgements in place, it can be argued that they remain deeply illusory on the utilitarian's view. When unpacked the judgement that I do wrong to a victim of homicide unless his or her death can be justified by reference to the victim's deserts contains a series of convenient fictions. To think that there is any objective (dis)value behind references to wronging someone, violating his or her rights, disregarding his or her deserts is to be mistaken. Using such notions will provide the right answers to moral questions in the real world. But the non-utilitarian is profoundly mistaken about the justification and objective reference of such notions. It appears indeed as if indirect utilitarianism gives good reason why most moral agents (those who do not need frequent recourse to critical thinking or a proper theory of justification) should continue to use notions delusive in content, though correct in outcome.

It may further by wondered how real is the justification given to ordinary thought by indirect utilitarianism. This justification consists in arguing that we know that utility will not be maximised by applying the theory directly to decisions for the most part but will be maximised by the majority acceptance of traditional moral principles. Inevitable defects in information gathering and processing justify this strategy. The problem for the utilitarian is to show how these defects do not also infect choices between two or more competing moral principles for direct use in making moral decisions (Frey 1984b:72–75). The utilitarian knows that in relying on non-utilitarian principles in decision making some utility will be foregone, for in principle if utilitarian calculations were made for each practical situation utility would be promoted. Not applying the theory directly can by justified if the limitations that beset information gathering and processing are stressed. But now these same important limitations will effect calculations of which set of non-utilitarian principles to choose for direct decision making. But here the utilitarian faces enormous problems. First there is in principle an untold number of possible moral rules to choose from as direct guides to action (Frey 1984b:73–4 and compare the discussion of rule utilitarianism above). Moreover the factors that effect choosing a general rule for a whole class of moral situations are greater in number and complexity than those for deciding the rights and wrongs of an individual case (Frey 1984b:74–5). In the former case one must consider not just actual, but possible and future, people and cases. It is difficult to avoid Frey's verdict that utility calculations of this sort remain at the level of vague guesses.

Such a conclusion leaves us with the thought that the justification given to the deliverances of the traditional conscience by indirect utilitarianism is spurious. This thought can be strengthened if we consider that much of the utility to be gained by sticking to traditional moral rules and considerations, and to be lost by seeking alternatives, is a simple function of the entrenched character of those rules and considerations. Consider, on either the classical or preference view, the dis-utility produced by a clear willingness to kill unrestrained by justice would in great measure be produced by the shocked expectations, anguish and moral confusion caused in members of a society who have a concern with justice and respect for life. Unless the utilitarian is actively concerned to shake people out of their non-utilitarian ways of moral thinking his concern to promote overall and long-term utility seems weak. If the utilitarian allows appeal to the theory's preferred modes of reasoning only in cases where traditional rules fail to produce a clear answer, the conservatism of theory may become too great for comfort. On both the classical and preference versions of the theory a great deal of dis-utility (in upset and disappointed preferences) would inevitably follow the attempt to reform a traditional society which regards women as semi-slaves.

CONCLUSION

I suggest that the attractiveness of utilitarianism lies in the promise of an idea, and not in its actual fulfillment. The promise is that of a 'scientific' and economical account of the nature and basis of moral judgement. The allure of that promise can be maintained only if the theoretical difficulties that the theory faces can be overcome. The promise will seem particularly worth pursuing if the alternatives to theory are seen as in terms of the following contrasts: first, intuition or prejudice in the making of moral decisions versus calculation based on empirical fact; and, second, mystery in the account of the source of value versus a simple picture of the basis of good.

This study is committed to rejecting these two contrasts. In describing the nature of moral reasoning I have been keen to stress the existence of informal modes of argument, of sharing and checking insight, which are removed from the scientific paradigm. I have also been concerned to show that there is at least one source of moral value in mundane reality, namely in the structure of human relationships. But this source is antithetical to the utilitarian portrayal of the basis of value. For if we accept the account offered in Chapter 2 we cannot think that people have interests, or pleasures and pains, in the first instance and then that moral rules arise at a second level out of the need to satisfy those interests in a harmonious way. Rather, the content and structure of people's interests is already formed by and dependent upon a realm of moral considerations which structures their lives. We shall return to this thought in Chapter 5.

5
Deontological Moral Theory

DEONTOLOGY AND ITS KANTIAN BASIS

Deontological moral theories are contrasted with teleological ones. The latter depend on or begin with an idea of the good and derive notions of right and wrong from that idea. Consequentialist moral theories are teleological, for they derive the rightness of an act from the good states of affairs it results in. Aretaic moral theories are teleological in a different manner. They contend that right acts are those which embody the human good, where this is thought of as the virtuous and best life. The differences between these forms of teleological theory will be further explored in Chapter 6, but either way they both relate rightness to a more basic idea of the good.

Deontological moral theories reverse this relationship between the good and the right. They hold that our foundational ideas of right and wrong can be worked out without any developed idea of the good, either as consequential goal of conduct or as a conception of the virtuous life. The independence and priority of the right over the good comes down to this: that there are some basic moral principles and rules in terms of which acts can be judged right and wrong and which can be justified independently of any developed idea of the good. Indeed, deontological theorists contend that we can only judge which goods are morally worthy of pursuit if we have some independent ideas of the right. Thus they stress the role of basic moral rules and principles as constraints on which goods we may pursue, in contrast, for example, to forms of direct utilitarianism which thinks of such rules as prescriptions for the most efficient promotion of goals.

The focus of a deontological theory is thus on foundational rules and the act species they define. These are the primary materials of moral thought. A proponent of such a theory will note that ordinary moral thought accepts and uses a stock of such rules, accepting them because they are a cultural 'given' and so obvious as to seem self-evident. Modern proponents of deontological theory cannot rest content with such a basis to foundational rules. They attempt to provide a philosophical deduction of such rules that all can accept and which will exhibit the rationality of basic rules. It cannot be a deduction which depends on a developed conception of the good (either as a goal to be realised as the consequence of action or as a form of life to be embodied in it). It cannot reason 'If we all agree that such-and-such is the goal of action we must obey these rules in order to attain it'. It appeals instead to the *form* of morality itself as making possible a deduction of moral rules. This idea of the form of morality is enriched by appeal to minimal conceptions of reason and the self which allegedly all will accept regardless of their conceptions of the good. With these enrichments, then we can produce a goal- and good-independent justification of foundational moral rules and neatly steer clear of the history of philosophical conflict over the good.

Many contemporary deontological theorists draw inspiration from the moral philosophy of Immanuel Kant. However, in so doing they sharply repudiate a feature of that philosophy which has come to be mistakenly associated with deontology itself. This is the idea that there are some moral rules which are valid absolutely, holding in any circumstances and come what may. Kant seems to have held this view about the rule 'Do not tell a deliberate untruth', contending that any lie was vicious, no matter what (Kant 1971:92–3). This absolutism is connected with another alleged feature of Kantian ethics, namely that it is purely formal, being based on the idea that moral rules can be judged valid or invalid without reference to empirical facts such as the consequences of obeying them. Out of this comes then a double characterisation of deontological ethics: it is absolutist about moral rules and rejects any appeal to empirical facts, such as consequences, in determining their validity.

These two alleged features of deontological thought can be made to appear decidedly unattractive. How can we be absolutists when we know that life is liable to throw up circumstances in which moral rules conflict? How can a sensible ethical theory tell us that basic moral rules can be deduced without reference to important areas of empirical fact?

Deontology cannot be dismissed so easily and by reference to a caricature of Kant's ethics. Kant was a moral rigorist, but his rigorism is now generally recognised to be independent of his ideas about the foundations of ethics. Those ideas do make essential reference to the form of morality but they do not exclude appeal to empirical fact, either in the working out of what are the basic moral rules or in decisions about how to act on these rules in particular cases. The key idea now taken from Kantian ethics by deontologists is that the process of using facts about human life and circumstances to work out valid moral rules need not rest on substantive views about the proper goal of conduct or the good life which should be embodied in it. The relevance and force of the facts we must appeal to is determined instead by features of morality, reason and the self which are common (because they are absolutely minimal) to all conceptions of the good. It is in this respect that Kantian ethics is formalist: it appeals in processing facts relevant to a code of morality to considerations which are independent of the content different people would give to statements of the goal to be pursued in conduct or of the ideal life to be embodied in it. The consequences of following one rule of conduct rather than another can be admitted as relevant in judging which rules are generally valid and how they are to be applied in particular cases. It is the *primacy* of consequences, particularly as granted by the idea that right is what promotes the best consequences, that deontological theory rejects. The right is not to be discovered by deciding in advance what the good is and then seeing what general policies would maximise that good.

Modern Kantian forms of deontology latch onto certain striking features of Kant's account of ethics and use these to provide a deduction of basic moral rules. They do not claim to interpret correctly, or use, all the many facets of Kant's writings on ethics, but by selecting and adapting some salient features of those writings they hope to give a rational reconstruction of morality. Using Green (1978) and Rawls (1972) I shall summarise this Kantian-derived deontology.

A starting point for authors such as Green and Rawls is Kant's rejection of what we might call the Classical endeavour to derive morality's structure and content from a determinate conception of the good life, particularly of the happy life. In the *Critique of Practical Reason* Kant has no problem with the thought that happiness is the goal of every rational individual and thus a key component in the human good (1956:63). However, the good so conceived will not lead directly to moral laws for two reasons. First we find that conceptions of what happiness consists in vary from individual to individual (1956:24–6). Second a determinate object of striving (such as academic success) thought of as leading to pleasure and happiness will only motivate if the subject has a prior desire for it (1956:19–20). But from these facts it follows that no universally binding rules, such as moral rules are conceived as being, can follow from a determinate conception of the good. There will be no agreement on what this good is and any particular candidate will be such that some find it desirable and part of their good while others will not. We will not be able to say that every one *ought* to pursue this good.

There is a strong hint in Kant's treatment of what he calls 'material objects of desire' that there can be no right or wrong, nothing rationally discussable, about the form they take. Which things I take pleasure and satisfaction in depends on the structure of my feelings of pleasure and is inevitably subjective (1956:20–4). Modern deontologists certainly build upon this idea. What, they assert, is common to us all is that we each have our own preferences and desires which define what is individually good for us. At the level of what we take our good to be there is no agreement and no prospect of rationally securing agreement. Hence, to establish basic moral rules we have to appeal to factors which are independent of the variety of human preferences and which build upon interests which all can be taken to have in common despite, or because of, that variety. We can summarise the deduction of a content for morality, as it appears in Green and Rawls, which builds upon these ideas, in terms of six key points.

1. Morality has a form as well as a content. If its form is properly and fully set out, it can be used to deduce its content once we add in some basic facts about human nature and circumstances. These facts and circumstances are not in themselves morally controversial or loaded.
2. The form of morality corresponds roughly to the definitional features outlined in chapter one. Morality is essentially a body of principles and rules which are impartial, universal and rational in character. They also provide the fundamental rules for social living and so are the final court of appeal for any clashes between the projects and preferences of society's members.
3. Morality should therefore embody the demands of rational impartiality in constructing a social order. All have reason

to accept its demands if they wish to be part of a rational, impartial social order.

4.   Morality can be thought of as resulting from an imaginary social contract. If we imagine a group of people devising rules for the ultimate ordering of a society in certain conditions, then, granted the conditions are properly worked out, whatever we see they must agree on as social rules will be the moral rules which we must all accept as having overriding force. The conditions must reflect the formal features of any moral order. Morality consists of universal principles, so no rule can be established in our imaginary setting unless it is agreed to by every one of the contractors. Moral rules are impartial. They favour no one's interests above an other's. To capture this feature we must imagine our contractors to have passed through 'a veil of ignorance' (Rawls 1972:136–42). Though the different members of the actual society will have different interests and talents, though some will be stronger than others, they are deprived before making out the contract of all knowledge of who they in fact are. They know only the basic facts of human nature and circumstances. Moral rules are rational. The contractors must decide on rules for their society on the basis of uncontroversial, practical rationality. What every one will agree on as a rational course for any actor is for him or her to seek to maximise the satisfaction of his or her preferences. So the contractors will decide on rules which give all the best opportunity of maximising the preference set they will end up with once the veil of ignorance is removed.

5.   In working out the contract the members of society need no shared ideas on what the good for human living and conduct is. Behind the veil of ignorance they know at least two facts about the good. One is that people's conceptions of it vary according to the preference set they have. The second is that the pursuit of these individual conceptions of the good is always likely to generate conflict between individuals. Given that they are constrained by the minimal conception of rationality granted to them (rational conduct is that which promotes preference satisfaction) and by the condition of impartiality, they cannot wait until leaving the veil of ignorance and then work out which conception of the good is 'correct', establishing moral rules in accord with this favoured conception. They can use generic facts about human

nature and circumstances to establish that there are certain minimal, neutral, *enabling* goods which a moral order will promote and reflect in its rules. These are goods which any of the contractors will find indispensable, regardless of which particular preference set they turn out to have. They include maximum liberty. All will find as much liberty as is socially possible a good given each has a unique preference set to pursue. Material prosperity of some kind will be important if plans of life are to be actively pursued. So will self-respect. But all-in-all only a 'thin' conception of the good is needed to found and launch morality.

6. What they will agree on is a set of rules which respects these 'thin' goods and which creates an impartial social order. They will be rules which bear upon clashes and conflicts between different individuals' pursuit of the good and which promote co-operation and self-esteem to make such pursuit more successful. So they will be rules protecting autonomy, forbidding violence upon others, enshrining fairness and honesty in contracts and bargains, and promoting forms of mutual aid and help.

Thus the contemporary re-working of the social contract fulfills the aims of deontology.

The social contract idea is intended to make sense of Kant's famous test of the Categorical Imperative, which is designed to tell us which acts are right through discovery of whether their maxims (that is, governing principles) are in accordance with the form of morality. The main formulation goes thus: 'So act that the maxim of your will could always hold at the same time as a principle establishing universal law' (Kant 1956:30). There is considerable controversy over the precise meaning of this test, not aided by the vagueness and vagaries in Kant's many examples of its application. It has been held to mean merely 'Think what it would be like if everyone acted thus'. So interpreted it is recognised to have little moral bite, but Green and others take it to mean something more, namely 'Would the rule behind your action be accepted by everyone else if offered as a binding principle of conduct?' There is evidence in the Kantian texts that this is how Kant understands it (Kant 1956:72, 1971:31 and 121, 1965:26 and 34). Construed in this way it might appear to yield a decision procedure for ethics. Suppose that I am tempted by my colleague's expensive new pen, carelessly left in my office. I consider taking it, effectively acting on the maxim 'Let me take what does not belong to me where this can be done in secret'. Now if this were openly put forward as one of the rules to guide social life too many would have too much to lose by it and too few too little to gain for it to stand any chance of being accepted by all. Thereby I know that the act is contrary to the claims of impartial right.

One of Kant's other formulations of the Categorical Imperative comes even closer to Rawls' and Green's deontology: 'Act so that you treat humanity, whether in your own person or in that of another, always as an end and never as a means only' (Kant 1959:47). This is held to mean testing whether one's act and maxim respects the existence of others as rational pursuers of their own plans of the good and thus their existence as equal partners in an impartial social order, with an indefeasible right to pursue their interests if such pursuit does not interfere with the preferences of other members of the social order. So I can see my maxim and act embodying secret theft does not respect my colleague's existence as an end in himself. It advances my preferences but only by depriving him of material goods, which in turn limits his ability to pursue his preferences. This is why we have rules protecting the property and persons of others, but why we should properly refrain from agreeing to social rules which restrain the pursuit of preferences which have no adverse effect on the ability of others to pursue their preferences. Thus interpreted Kant chimes in with the concern of modern social contract theorists to set as a general goal the maximising of individual liberty for a just society: 'Justice is the aggregate of those conditions under which the will of one person can be conjoined with the will of another in accordance with the universal law of freedom' (Kant 1965:34).

EXPLORING THE SOCIAL CONTRACT

Thus far my brief sketch of contemporary deontological theory has intended to get across its general shape and its claim to have provided a uniquely sound justification of basic moral rules. The soundness of this deduction is held to lie in the way it employs allegedly non-controversial defining features of morality, non-controversial empirical facts about human life and its circumstances, and an account of reason in conduct which is the least loaded and question begging on offer. Moral rules are judged to be those which embody a minimal rationality (interpreted as a desire to secure maximal satisfaction of preferences). This minimal rationality is constrained merely by the impartiality and universality derived from the essence of morality, on the one hand, and by the basic facts about the tendency of plans of life to conflict in practice, on the other, facts which make it advantageous to have universally binding and impartial principles for regulating clashes between preferences.

A justification of moral rules along these lines would be a remarkable success if social contract/deontological theory had really established it. There are a range of problems with the attempt which can be brought out even from our brief sketch of the theory.

One obvious problem with the imaginary social contract is to see how it has any binding force on members of an actual society. Its description is best seen as a vivid way of setting out how determinate moral judgements can be reached if the proper constraints embodied in the ideas of morality and reason are respected. It does not follow from the model that actual members of actual societies have a motive to obey moral rules. At most the model shows that most people have much to gain from there being an impartial way of coping with conflicts of interest between members of society. So that it is a good that there is such thing as a moral order. But it does not show that the individual who thinks he or she can take advantage of this order by benefiting from the restraint of others, while secretly disobeying moral rules where personal advantage accrues, is acting irrationally. Indeed, the conception of rationality as maximising preference satisfaction makes this particular problem of justification in morality *more* difficult, since it implies that it is rational to obey moral principles only if my actual preferences are thereby maximised.

Some proponents of re-worked Kantian deontology think this problem so serious as to demand Kant's solution to a similar difficulty: namely the postulation of a non-human form of justice in the universe that will guarantee that only those who respect rules of right and are thus worthy to be happy will in the end enjoy happiness defined as the maximal satisfaction of preferences. (Thus Green 1978, particularly chapter three, re-uses Kant's moral proof of the existence of God. His arguments on this score will be considered in Chapter 7 below.)

Consideration of the character of the hypothetical contract in

Rawls and his followers also indicates that the theory is not really contractarian. To be such it must show how moral and social rules are the product of human agreement and bargain. But there is no agreeing and bargaining in the initial position behind Rawls' and Green's contract. The separateness of the selves who are contracting has been dissolved with the veil of ignorance. They have identical, because generic, interests and knowledge. There is no bargaining to be done in such circumstances.

It may also be doubted whether they are in reality constrained to opt for the fair-minded rules of right that the morally sound would favour. Rawls, for example, is famous for arguing that the intuition that the talented and strong and powerful should see their advantages as in the first instance a benefit to society at large will be honoured by his contractors. So they will accept a principle which allows folk to enjoy the fruits of their greater endowments only if the position of the weakest is thereby bettered (through, for example, increasing society's general wealth). The puzzle, aired by many commentators, is that on minimal economic rationality it cannot be unreasonable for anyone to adopt a policy of 'everyone look after his own and the devil take the hindmost' unless such a policy is non-preference maximising for those who consider it. According to the model, the original contractors will have too much anxiety about the chance of turning out to be a poorly endowed weakling to agree to any such aggressive but risky social rule. But it may be equally (or more) rational to agree to take such risk, given that the rewards will be so much higher (Brown 1986:60–62).

The underlying objection here is that the notions of rationality and impartiality employed in the theory are too thin to produce the deduction of the required principles and that if more is added the model will be seen to depart from its alleged neutrality and impartiality among different conceptions of the worthwhile life. It would be a mjor blow to the modern re-working of deontology if it turned out to employ substantive ideas of the good in the deduction of basic moral rules. That there are substantive principles of the good at work may be alleged once we reflect on what the model employed understands by respect for persons. The model bids us to respect each individual as an end in him or herself. This is held to be equivalent to respecting each as the holder of a unique preference set and licensing restrictions on the satisfaction of those preferences only if their pursuit would materially interfere with others' pursuit of their preferences. So creating the maximal set of liberties emerges as an essential goal of any worthwhile moral outlook, because it is entailed by the essence of morality and the very way in which moral rules can be justified.

The critic can surely argue that whether this is the right way to measure respect for persons, or whether the assertion of the value liberty to pursue an individual preference is correct, cannot be made true by definition. We can imagine moral outlooks which have different ideas of respect for persons and which do not place such a high value on liberty as conceived by the contractarian. Consider the strict sabbatarian who argues that disrespect for the Lord's Day is so serious a harm for individuals and society that all should be obliged to refrain from work and public pleasure on a Sunday. This individual values persons in so far as they are prospective candidates for salvation. Securing their liberty to act as they please is of comparatively little value if that liberty is exercised in ways that are detrimental to their basic good, as he sees it. Now it would appear that what we have here is a substantive disagreement over matters of the good: the high value of liberty to pursue individual life style, as some see it, versus the high value on salvation and corporate acknowledgement of religious obligation, as others see it. How can this disagreement be settled by legislation based on the form of morality? By the same token, it will not do to say that the evil of Sabbath breaking represents an evil for some merely in respect of it going against their preference sets, so their perception cannot be used as the basis of a social rule. For to characterise the status of 'evil' as merely that which is contrary to a preference set is already to contend that the sabbatarian's world view is *false*. If the matter is characterised thus then already a large part of this individual's conception of the good has been set aside. If the contractors in the original position are told that, yes, they may end up being people with certain religious outlooks, but that they do not have to consider seriously the truth of these outlooks in framing the contract (because all such outlooks are private visions which can only be prosecuted between people in entirely voluntary association), then they are given a positive ideology in framing the contract. It is that of secular, contemporary liberalism.

It seems odd to want to make this outlook true by reference to the essence of morality. On the surface our sabbatarian can honour the three defining features of morality that figure so largely in the deontologist's theory. He may claim all the following to be true of it. The rule against Sabbath breaking can be commended universally: there are reasons which all could in principle accept which lie behind it. It is in consequence based on reason: to reject it is irrational given where our good evidently lies. It is impartial. It does not elevate a person's or group's preferences as a norm for others, because the evil of Sabbath breaking is independent of *anyone's* preferences.

My suggestion is that we must engage in substantive argument about the truth and evidential status of particular visions of the good to settle debates about the appropriateness of different pre-scriptions for social living. We should not hide substantive decisions about the good in procedural devices.

It is evident from our example that liberal, contractarian theorising has problems with those people who have preferences about the behaviour of others. Many people do value forms of social solidarity, corporate behaviour and witness, and the existence of traditional institutions. Not all of these forms of corporate life can survive translation into a society where all associations are entirely vol-untary and the outcome of bargains between individual sets of preferences. Now the contractarian would be much happier with individuals whose preference sets dealt only in individual goods, that is goods attainable through individual effort alone or through voluntary association with others. Preference sets which contain desires for how others act and satisfy their preferences upset the apple cart. Decisions about how to strike a balance between the preferences of individuals cannot then be represented as ones to do with maximising a neutral value – liberty – or about minimising an uncontroversial evil – conflict and preference dissatisfaction.

These points can be stengthened by consideration of the conten-tion that the ideal of creating the greatest possible set of liberties is incoherent (for the argument that follows see O'Neill 1980). It is part of the modern contractarian deontologist's outlook that this ideal can be pursued in practice without appealing to standards of the good in deciding which liberties are to be allowed and which constrained. It is the maximal set of liberties we are after. Thus our only rule in deciding which liberties to allow and which to constrain is 'liberty may be constrained only for the sake of securing a more extensive liberty'. But there is no such thing as the most extensive liberty. Virtually any social rule can present itself as constraining liberty for the sake of liberty. The sabbatarian's rules restrict liberty to work on a Sunday for the sake of creating the liberty to live in a society which respects the Lord's Day. But, it may be objected, his rule cannot be said to create the most extensive set of liberties. To reason in this way, however, we need to have a means of counting liberties, so that we can judge one set to be larger than another. Liberties to do actions can be individuated in different ways, following from the diverse ways of identifying actions: 'If so, it would always be possible to show that any given set of liberties was as numerous as any other merely be listing the component liberties more specifically' (O'Neill 1980:50). Moreover any set of liberties automatically rules out a contrary set. A set of liberties which allows women the liberty to wander the streets unmolested restricts the liberties of rapists to pursue their pleasures. We won't find a largest set of liberties by looking for one that includes as many liberties as possible and excludes as few as possible – given that to each set of liberties there will be a contrary set.

It seems that when we make comparisons between the amount of liberty this social order allows compared with that, we employ tacit principles of relevance and importance for selecting what are worthwhile liberties. We no doubt think of *important* freedoms connected with our idea of human dignity and the human good which are counted first in comparing systems of liberty. Hence, if we have no principles other than those which tell us to create the greatest amount of liberty we will be at a loss to know where to begin counting. The pursuit of liberty is the pursuit of the kinds of liberty worth having on some view or other of human nature, diginity and good. Without such a view the injunction to create the greatest possible liberty is empty.

The suggestion is that contemporary deontological theory carries a heavy ideological load. It will produce a morality which satisfies the aspirations of modern liberal individualism and that outlook's conception of the good life and of worthwhile liberties. But does the fact that the minimal conception of rationality and the particular interpretation of impartiality used by deontological theory leads to this conception of the good life in any way establish the truth of the liberal outlook?

The fact that the contractarian structure is morally controversial is sealed by the recognition that on its terms it is hard to see how such creatures as human infants, the unborn, the severely mentally handicapped and animals can be moral subjects. Not being capable of articulating and pursuing a preference set they are not partakers of the social contract and cannot enjoy the respect owed to those who have plan of life that is uniquely their own. So Gauthier, articulating the contractarian tradition, states 'Animals, the unborn, the congenitally handicapped and defective, fall beyond the pale of morality tied to mutuality' (Gauthier 1986:268). Yet again there are important substantive questions (about the extent and nature of moral obligation beyond adult, rational subjects) to be explored here. We simply cannot have our answers prejudged by procedural decisions about the most economic assumptions concerning morality's and reason's essence needed for the purposes of moral enquiry.

Some of the difficulties explored so far are peculiar to Rawlsian, neo-Kantian versions of the deontological, contractarian idea. Others pertain to all versions of the contemporary project of deducing the right while consigning questions about the good to individual preference sets.

Gauthier, for example, contends that contractarian ethics works without Rawl's hypothetical contract and its original position. In his study *Morals by Agreement* he presents a case for saying that the essence of contractarianism is that principles of right are created by human agreement. Thus a deontological outlook is correct: these principles are not derived from substantive goods. The agreement in question has none of the mystery of Rawls' and Green's fictional founding of society. It is an agreement repeated in substance in the actual ways rational individuals make trade offs between each other's interests in the present. In essence Gauthier's contractarian deontology has the following elements (see Gauthier 1986:8–19). It contains a 'minimal' conception of the good and of rationality. These are based upon the familiar ideas that people have sets of preferences which establish some things as good and evil for them and make it rational for them to seek to maximally satisfy these preferences. People need to bargain with others to secure this rational goal, both because preference sets conflict in practice and because some preferences require the cooperation of others to be fulfilled. Rationality as preference maximisation requires society to exist as a cooperative venture for mutual advantage. In practice (and here the complexities of Gauthier's analysis of how to maximise the chances of personal advantage in cooperative ventures can be ignored), individuals can best enhance their chances of advantageous cooperation with others if they internalise certain constraints on the pursuit of preference satisfaction. These constraints are the principles of morality and it is in this way that they are justified. They are rational constraints on the pursuit of direct preference maximisation by rational individuals because they work to the mutual advantage of those individuals.

As we might expect there are objections to the technical aspects of Gauthier's attempted demonstration that even the strong and cunning have reason, on his analysis of 'reason', to obey moral constraints. Once more these doubts turn around whether the contractarian account builds so little into the initial sources of morality as to justify even the moral rules he or she would recognise as valid (compare Sumner 1987:156–62). If we waive such thoughts, our attention will turn to whether there are other valid rules of right which the contractarian cannot justify and whose importance shows that the entry point into morality is too narrow. We have seen that Gauthier's method rules out of existence any rationally defensible moral rules which enshrine obligations to subjects who cannot act as rational bargainers of interests. Does not the fact that we would all recognise the existence of at least some such obligations show that his starting points for the rational defence of morality, far from being minimal and uncontroversial, is fatally flawed? In Gauthier's eyes his initial assumptions about reason and the good are unproblematic because following from the way in which contemporary economic theory reasons about human action. But might not our considered moral judgements show that it was incorrect to take what is adequate in one, partial, study of human action and apply it to another?

Gauthier is insulated to some extent from this kind of argument, because he roundly denies the power of 'intuitions' to overthrow theory, comparing the matter to the scientist's refusal to let his theories be dictated to by pre-scientific, popular belief (1986:269). We have questioned this account of the relation between judgement and theory in Chapter 2. Leaving aside, for the moment, the adequacy of his account of rationality and the good in the light of our considered moral judgements , we may note that Gauthier's moral theory is strikingly individualist in its starting points and methods. This is not the same as selfish or egoistic. Gauthier need not deny that we have by nature and upbringing interests in others. But he needs morality to grow out of a set of interests whose existence is not predicated on the existence of other peoples's interests. People acquire joint interests with others. Contractarian theory merely has to explain how such mutual interests grow out of separate interests of the persons concerned which are intelligible prior to the fact of relationship and mutual involvement. Hence, the primary moral relationship for the contractarian is the free bargain, where each party has identifiable interests prior to the bargain and can reason that these interests will be furthered if considerations are exchanged with the other parties. These interests may be interests in others, so the rational contractor is not necessarily a selfish egoist. He or she is a 'non-tuist' (Gauthier 1986:311). The non-tuist has a range of interests which exist prior to relationship with others and can therefore reason whether these interests are furthered by entering into moral relationships with others. So all sharing of interests with others in moral relationship is likened to a bargain – an exchange of promises on consideration of mutual advantage. Bargaining presupposes that I should be able to identify my interest, my advantage, prior to the fact of relationship the bargain establishes.

We owe it to Gauthier to reveal so clearly the individualism (note, again, I do not say 'egoism') on which so much modern moral theory rests. There are two chief objections to this individualism: it offers a fantastic account of many forms of social relationship and it impoverishes our conception of the individual.

The first of these criticisms can be attached to the following words of Gauthier:

> The liberal individual does not lack emotional ties to other persons, but those she has are of her own volition, or more properly, represent the joint volition of the persons tied. Just as each individual has her own conception of the good, and makes her own choice among possible ways of life, so each individual makes her own choice of others as objects of affection. She is not bound by fixed social roles, either in her activities or in her feelings. Although social affective relationships are essential to the liberal individual, there are no essential social relationships. (Gauthier 1986:347)

This puts one in mind of the statement in a well-known liberal defence of abortion that we only have obligations to others if we have freely chosen those obligations (so a mother-to-be has no obligations to an unwanted fetus, parents to an unwanted baby; Thompson 1986:17–18). These are fantastic accounts of the basis of many social relationships and obligations. Do the parents of a handicapped child have no obligations to it if they have done all in their power not to have a handicapped infant? Does a child have no obligations to sick and elderly parent if he or she has not chosen to accept them? In general what would it be like to think of all of the social ties that enmesh one (to parents, spouse, children, siblings, fellow citizens, one's country, one's neighbours) as the objects of choice? In many instances the commitment to the daily duties that such relationships entail (consider all that a parent does over the years for a child) would be unsustainable if it was thought of as resting on nothing other than choice, rewarded perhaps by reciprocal benefit.

The further difficulty in casting all obligation-creating relationships after the model of a freely chosen bargain is that it leads to a questionable account of the self that lies behind these relationships. To make Gauthier's idea of the liberal individual intelligible we must think of he or she weighing up, in terms of extant interests, whether to be connected to this person in that relationship. This entails that there must be an intact self, capable of making bargains and considering the worth of entering into relationships, in abstraction from participation in these relationships. This self must be able to put to itself the question 'Given my preferences is it worth my being tied in this relationship to this person?' But as we noted in Chapter 2, the fact about moral relationships is that many are essential for the constitution of a self. They give the person involved a set of extended personal interests (Harrison 1989). In abstraction from these interests there would be precious little of a self remaining to have any developed ideas of what was and was not worth bargaining for. Consider what would be the range of interests that constitute your self if you abstracted from it all those interests which now depend on the 'social effective relationships' that help to constitute your life. What is left of you if you are considered in abstraction from being a citizen of a particular country, a child of these parents, a sibling, a spouse, a colleague of these people?

A large part of what constitutes a particular individual and his or her interests will be given by the ties and relationships he or she has with others. This is why, though such relationships have a moral structure and underpinning, bargain or contract is not a good model for it. The liberal individual required by contractarian deontology can be accused of bearing little resemblance to the actual self that is a moral agent in the real world. And a morality which suits this individual may bear little resemblance to one that suits actual people. (Similar and very detailed criticisms of the self behind Rawlsian contract theory can be found in Sandel 1982.)

PREFERENCES AND THE GOOD

Contemporary deontological theories appear to capture well some aspects of the moral life. Some of ordinary morality fits in well with the aim of securing an impartial order in which each may pursue his or her interests or engage in bargains with others for mutual advantage. Its claim to be *the* account of morality rests upon its ideas about good and preference. If good is simply the product of preference and if there can in consequence be no rational, moral enquiry into different conceptions of the good, then, failing the truth of some form of preference utilitarianism, there can be nothing more to morality than the creation of the kind of social order that the contractarian favours. Both contractarians and preference utilitarians favour the subjectivity of value described in Chapter 1. Both endeavour to rescue some measure of objectivity and rationality for morality despite that subjectivity. Both agree that the good for an individual just is what a given preference set happens to determine. They differ in how the good of individuals is to be counted in working out principles of right. The contractarian picture depends on the subjectivity of the good. Because principles and rules of right cannot derive from objective good, so they can be seen as the product of collective choice and agreement (Sumner 1987:152–4). There is no rational way of deriving rules from substantive views about the good. Rationality resides only in working out individual utilities and the trade-offs we are prepared to make with others in that process. The rationality of morals must be that of a grand bargain for the contractarian.

Now if we reject the vision of the good and of practical rationality enshrined in this subjectivity of values we have reason to question the deontologist's picture of morality. First there will be an area of genuine moral reflection excluded from the contractarian's limiting of discussion to 'morality in the narrow sense'. The contractarian will be omitting those aspects of ethics which concern '"the art of life", that is, the precepts instructing people as to how to live and what makes for a successful, meaningful and worthwhile life' (Raz 1984:57). Second the contractarian will exclude a range of moral comment on the worthwhileness of certain preference pursuits. If there are objective, rationally discussable goods independent of preference, then the value of allowing freedom to pursue some preferences may be more than offset by the disvalue of the object of those preferences. Our strict sabbatarian reasons thus about the value of being free to dishonour the Lord's Day. Many feminists reason thus about the value of being free to purchase and enjoy pornography. Readers should be able to think of their own examples. In these and other ways, it might be argued that contractarian deontology cannot give sufficient account of ethics and that only an account which is prepared to admit that there are rationally justifiable goods independent of preference can.

So much hangs on the account of preference, reason and the good which is at the heart of much contemporary moral philosophy that we cannot accept its validity on the spurious grounds that it is the minimum we need for a theory of ethics, or that it is the one that dominates economics and social science. The question must be asked: 'Is it adequate to the range of experience and judgement arising from the moral life?' I believe that there is an array of recent commentary upon it that shows it to be fundamentally flawed (as in Bond 1983, Brown 1983, Dent 1984, Finnis 1983, Hollis 1987, McNaughton 1988, Sumner 1981 and 1987). I shall try to get the main points of this critical commentary across.

The preference view of good threatens to sever what is good from human happiness and welfare. For having a prior preference for an object is neither a sufficient nor a necessary condition for finding that attainment of it is satisfying, rewarding, enjoyable. It is not sufficient for there is no commoner human experience than that of attaining an object of desire and discovering that it brings no contentment. It is not necessary for we frequently find that happiness comes from experience of states that we had not previously desired. Preference theorists endeavour to overcome these objections by contending that it is only *informed* or *reflective* desires whose satisfaction brings happiness. But while misinformation about the consequences of fulfilling a desire can sometimes explain the facts we refer to, it is frequently only the experience of the objects of our desires that shows us that they are not satisfying, enjoyable, worthwhile, and so forth. Referring to 'informed desires' is shown to be a mere epicycle of the theory by the fundamental fact that it is through experience human beings learn what is satisfying and what is not.

The preference view has problems in explaining how I should be concerned about my future happiness. It appears, on the model, to be rational to think about future well being only if I have present preferences that connect my desiring self at the moment to my desiring self in the future. Further epicycles have to be added to cope with this difficulty. If there is value independent of preference, there is a continuing order of values to which I can relate a concern for my future good.

The preference view promises a fantastic account of good and evil. It is hard to believe that whatever is the object of a preference is thereby a good or that a good life consists in having one's preferences satisfied. We would not say of someone, who through limited and oppressive upbringing had a very limited and distorted range of desires, that they attained the good even if it should turn out that they want what they get and get what they want. This appears to ignore the importance of reflection on how someone gains his or her desires and on what modes of life they make possible. The conditioned and brain-washed citizens of Huxley's *Brave New World* are in the state of getting what they want and wanting what they get. It is hard to believe that evil in human life consists only in the frustration of desire and that nothing can be a human evil unless it has frustrated a desire.

The preference view suggests an impoverished account of self-respect. It appears unable to account for this phenomenon (which many reflective folk experience at some stages in their lives): I know what my plans and preferences are, but I lose faith in their worth and the worth of the self that has them. I ask myself 'Why do I matter and why do the things that I pursue matter?' My ability and freedom to pursue my preferences may not be in question. I want to know in my self doubt and despair why it matters one way or the other whether this ability and freedom is exercised. Such questions seem unintelligible and unresolvable unless I have a sense that there are objective goods that I may compare my projects with. A sense of self-worth relates in part to the recognition that some of the projects pursued and fulfilled in the past represent genuine achievements. It can be restored through this recollection and a sense that what is aimed at now is capable of being recognised by others as valuable, of making a genuine addition to the stock of the world's goods. The value of the individual and the individual's freedom relates to the value of what that individual pursues. They are underpinned by the possibility of social recognition of the worth of what one pursues. This thought suggests a social foundation for the good of freedom. It also hints that, far from the idea of the free pursuit of preference being the foundation of morality, the existence of a moral order which includes the social acknowledgement of a range of human goods is the foundation for a worthwhile freedom.

Developing these thoughts leads us back to a contention advanced earlier in this study: that many preferences presuppose, rather, than create, a perceived value in their object and are unintelligible without that underlying perception of value. Some desires are rationally induced. They arise out of a prior belief, whether generated by reflection or experience, that their objects are in some respect or other worthwhile. Others, while arising unreflectively, depend on values predicated in their objects. My fear in the face of some threat may arise unbidden by reason, but it is answerable in principle to my judgement that the threat in reality poses no danger to me. For very many preferences the preference theory of value reverses the proper relation between preference and value: preferences are created by or answerable to judgements of value, rather than the other way around.

The above view about the preference-value relation promises a better, clearer idea of how practical reason functions. It makes some sense to say that rationality in conduct consists in satisfying as many of one's desires as possible, where 'desires' refers to definite and settled plans and already presupposes that a range of practical goals has been agreed upon, the only question being the technical one of how many and in which order I should act upon. But where 'desire' means felt preference it is not at all clear how the model of rationality as the maximal satisfaction of desire works, not least because it seemingly eliminates reflection on the score of whether my felt preference is for something that is worthy of pursuit.

On the view of value as preference independent I can reason about which preferences I shall pursue by considering the degree of good in the objects of those references. I can engage in public and private reflection about the comparative worth of the things I am initially inclined to pursue. I reason and reflect about the objects of my preferences. This looks to be the way in which we do in fact consider what to do. On the preference view of value I must look away from the objects I might choose to the structure of my preferences, considering which preferences, if satisfied, would lead to the abandonment of the least number of other extant preferences I have and which preferences are stronger than others. Strength of preference becomes crucial on this account, but also mysterious. I cannot tell whether my preference for going to the pub every evening is stronger than my preference for helping with the family by asking which I judge to be more worthwhile overall. I either have to accept my own private opinion poll that, faced with a choice between them I just find myself preferring a situation in which one is satisfied rather than another, or I must somehow weigh their respective psychological force. It appears astonishing to suggest that I might decide which of two incompatible desires like these I should act upon by reflecting on which gives me the greater urge or itch.

Preference theorists sometimes bring in the notion of second-order preferences, that is preferences about preferences, to explain how there can be some reflective structure to decisions about which preferences to satisfy. So if I have developed a second-order preference for obeying family duties and against automatic indulging in sensual pleasure, I can settle my clash between the desires for beer and helping to put the children to bed by reference to that second-order preference. There are two things wrong with this escape route. We still have a mystery about how second-order preferences arise. If they just represent awareness of habits of choice between preferences that we have built up in the course of life then the problem about how choices between preferences are ever made is still there. Further it is hard to see how on the preference view of value they could be decisive (as argued by Hollis 1987:42). A second-order preference against beer drinking and for the duties of fatherhood increases by one the number of preferences whose satisfaction I forgo if i opt for the pub. But whatever I do will be accompanied by an awareness of a number of contingently unsatisfiable preferences. Why merely because this is a preference about a preference should it be decisive? On the preference view of value it can only be the strength of the preference that could make it decisive, but then I might still find the preference for beer drinking, accompanied by unsatisfied second-order preferences against indulging myself, psychologically stronger. Then I act rationally if I go to the pub. My second-order preference *can* be decisive if it represents the reflective judgement, that though beer drinking is fun, it is less worthwhile, less valuable as an activity, than the exercise of family duties.

The view of practial rationality flowing from the preference view of value is wholly instrumental. Ends are set by given preferences. Reasoning about ends is possible only to the extent that not all preferences are of the same 'strength' and they are not all consistently satisfiable in the real world. Fundamentally, however, rationality is to do with efficiency in the pursuit of goals set independently of reason by preference. What this portrait ignores is the experience familiar from countless occasions of the exercise of practical reason of modifying our goals as we learn what is involved in pursuing them. It is a mark of practical stupidity to pursue a goal come what may when that pursuit has shown it not be worthwhile. The preference theorist can only allow learning about the need to modify and abandon ends to include discovery that pursuit of one preference-elected goal is incompatible with other preference-elected goals. This is once more arbitrarily to set limits to the operation of reason and the range of experience in defence of a dogma. It is a mark of practical wisdom to be open as far as possible to the lessons of reflection and experience that are there to be learnt from the actual paths we must follow to pursue our goals.

In summarising reasons for rejecting the preference view of value I have given admittedly only one side of a continuing debate in contemporary philosophy. However, it is enough for my purposes if this and earlier discussions in this study establish a case for taking a contrary, objective view of value seriously. It is this view of value that aretaic moral value depends upon and it needs to be taken seriously for aretaic theory to be worthy of consideration.

6

Aretaic Moral Theory

THE STRUCTURE OF THE GOOD LIFE

We have introduced an aretaic moral theory so far as one that derives the rightness of right acts from the correctness of the motives that lie behind them. In the history of moral philosophy this idea comes down to the following: there are certain excellences of human character -- the virtues – and praiseworthy conduct is that which flows from a life which manifests these excellences. A life which manifests the virtues is one which displays the human good, which shows human flourishing or happiness to the highest degree. A virtue is a habit of choice and it is in this rarified sense of 'motive' that we can say an act is right if it is done for the right motive – meaning an act is right if it is one that a person displaying the human good would choose.

Aretaic theory is a form of non-consequentialist telelogy. It is teleological in shaping ethics around the idea of an ultimate goal or end: the achievement of the human good or flourishing. A notion of what this end is provides the ultimate organising point around which moral thought coheres. It is not consequentialist for two reasons. First the relation between the ultimate good it posits and choiceworthy action is not that such action leads to or causally promotes ultimate good. Since the human good consists in a life manifesting the virtues, the relation between the good and right action consists in such action displaying character traits, which are habits of choice. It follows that specific right acts do not merely lead to the good – they manifest it directly. If they are the means to the realisation of the good, it is in the philosopher's sense of being *constitutive means*. From this we see that aretaic moral theory can accept that acts may be inherently right or wrong, for the ultimate good is itself a mode of activity which acts can succeed or fail in manifesting. A second ground for saying that aretaic theory is non-consequentialist is that it offers no hope that reasoning about how to promote and display the human good could be reduced to the application of a rule concerned with the calculation of numerically measurable good consequences. The aretaic theorist may speak of better and worse in relation to actions, lives and manifestations of the good. But such talk is not to be translated into comparison of a variable that can be measured independently of moral judgement.

In this specific respect the different virtues that make up the human good are incommensurable. If it were otherwise, if consequentialism were true, we could give someone the knowledge required to be a good human being by giving him or her a general principle which provided the means of calculating the better and worse of how to promote and manifest the good. The virtues would be ultimately reducible to a single virtue, that concerned with working out and acting upon this single measure of the good. The chief author of aretaic theory, Aristotle, makes it quite plain that this is impossible when he asserts that practical wisdom is inseperable from goodness. Only one who has acquired the virtues through action and experience can be practically wise (Aristotle 1925a:1144b).

It follows from all that has been said so far that aretaic theory must have quite different pretensions from the other forms of contemporary moral theory we have treated. Both consequentialist and deontological theories seek a decision procedure or algorithm for ethics. They wish moral philosophy, a theoretical enterprise undertaken by people of probably limited goodness and certainly limited practical experience, to validate principles which are clear and certain enough to be the basis of ethical decision making. Part of what is meant by saying that acts are correct if proceeding from right habits of choice (the virtues) is that no principles can be a substitute for excellence of choice acquired through practice (or at least no principles that are clear-cut enough to be applied without the skill and judgement that is part of being practically wise and which can only be learnt with the experience of making choices). This is why this study is biased toward aretaic theory. Aretaic theory accords with the moral epistemology outlined in Chapters 1 to 3 and with the limited role to moral philosophy that epistemology provides. Aristotle's emphasis on practical wisdom's connection with goodness and on virtues as habits of choice entails the 'bottom-up' account of moral knowledge we have favoured. If such knowledge results ultimately in right habits of choice and traits of character then there is a presumption that it will primarily be built up from experience of moral reality gained in making choices. It also implies that, as suggested by our earlier account, moral experience will be social. The training of perception and choice that is involved in acquiring it will necessarily rely on others, both directly (for their wisdom and experience) and indirectly as the means by which one tests one's own judgements.

Griffin complains of moral theories which stress the virtues that they are of little practical use. Even with a worked out theory of this type we cannot settle the big moral questions such as 'When is abortion licit?'. Such theories are formal, without real moral content.

> Getting our motivation in good order is a large part of the moral battle. But it is only a part. We also need answers to certain central questions. (Griffin 1986:64)

In part this complaint is sound but irrelevant, in part it is unsound. We have seen that is of the essence of a virtues-based account of moral reasoning and goodness, that no moral philosophy could answer 'the big moral questions' for us. At best it might contribute to an answer. The complaint of virtues theory's emptiness is decisive only if there is an alternative philosophical theory which would answer the big questions, that is if the rival claims to have a decision procedure for ethics were correct. In part this complaint is unsound, for virtue theory means something substantial and highly ramified by its assertion that right acts proceed from right motives. In consequence, as we shall see below, it has things to offer on how moral reasoning should be structured. Informed by it we might have much to say on the reasons provided for various social polcies.

According to a plausible account of aretaic theory moral knowledge will begin with experience, aided by others, of which features of circumstances are morally relevant and which acts are choiceworthy. Such experience will suggest rough clasess of action which are right, wrong or permissible. This knowledge may be summed up in terms of rules. It will build up into a sense of which patterns of choice and activity are worthy of praise and condemnation and thus yield a picture of the virtues and vices which can be displayed in conduct. Knowledge that so-and-so is a virtue may be expressed in terms of the truth of a general principle. Completeness and order in our knowledge of the virtues and of principles now leads us to think about how the various virtues are to be ranked. Experience and reflection make us aware that different virtues, such as kindness and justice, conflict in various situtations. Habits of choice expressive of practical wisdom will extend to ways of responding to such conflicts through ordering the virtues. It is central to aretaic theory that it recommends that thought about such ranking be structured around the key idea of the best, most noble way of life which, with good fortune, we can imagine a person living. This conception bids us to consider the question of what order to place the human virtues in by considering what shape a life which exhibited each to the best degree would look like. Here we might think of the problem in terms of education (compare Scruton 1986:326–7). If we had the task of instructing a child in the best life to lead and thought about the child as having a reasonable span of life with a reasonable amount of external and material fortune, what overall shape to its life would we wish to commend? We would have to think of what overall way of life would best commend itself as the way in which this individual could flourish as a human being. And in thinking of this we would naturally have to take stock of the thought that some of the virtues would conflict some of the time. Thus we are lead into thinking how they are to be ordered and ranked.

The idea of the human good, that of the unqualifiedly best mode of human living, is meant to provide in aretaic theory the final target of ethical reflection which introduces the necessary coherence into it. Once we reach this stage of moral thought we may see how moral experience connects with other areas of human knowledge. In thinking through our conception of the human good we will have to be aware of what other sources of reflection and experience tell us about the character of human nature and circumstances. Our religion, metaphysics or general philosophy will give us ideas about the characteristic and important human powers we should expect any worthwhile life to display. They will tell us of how we conceive of the reality in which these powers are to be displayed.

In this way there can be 'top-down' reasoning in ethics, as we are invited by such considerations to view the human good as having a certain character, and through this down to what the virtues might be and ultimately what acts are right. Equally the aretaic model helps us to conceive how 'bottom-up' reasoning helps us to mould and modify such general conceptions of human nature and circumstances. It provides for the fullest integration between non-moral and moral knowledge. It allows for there being distinct levels of moral thought each of which is capable of contributing to moral knowledge. We have knowledge of: acts (and with them act-types and rules), commendable motives and habits of choice, human virtues and vices (and with them general principles of conduct), an order or ranking of the virtues, and finally the best, most praiseworthy and desirable form of human life: the good for human beings. If aretaic theory disclaims some of the pretensions of other philosophical theories of ethics and insists on our experience of the first layer – choices of acts and the morally relevant circumstances in which they are made – it is because of its perception of ethics as a practical discipline. The goal of ethics is knowledge of how to choose and act. Knowledge of how to choose and act cannot be reduced to knowledge of rules, still less of principles. Rules and principles stand some way above choice and action, since they cannot themselves tell us: how to correctly see the situations to which they are applicable, how to interpret them, when to modify or set them aside as circumstances demand. Habits of choice do not suffer from these defects and that is why philosophical reflection that matters should centre around what habits of choice are praiseworthy, and how they are interrelated in a mode of living that is the best (compare Aristotle 1925b:1216^b and Hutchinson 1986:2–3).

One of the claimed advantages for aretaic moral theory is that it provides an understanding of how its rivals function and how their claims are to be justified, which they in turn cannot provide of it:

> the theory can find a place within the framework, and it can therefore explain, other and conflicting theoretical frameworks which cannot in turn find a place for it. Other theories of morality . . . can be expressed within this framework, as prescribing ways of which give differing priorities to essential virtues and to differing powers of mind and habits of action. (Hampshire 1977:16)

Contemporary deontological theory can be seen to give essential priority to justice as a virtue, conceiving this to consist in fairness toward others, honesty in bargains and contracts and respect for the autonomy of others. The best kind of life is one in which this paramount virtue is manifested along with the skill and material prosperity necessary to maximally satisfy one's preferences. Aretaic theories influenced by Aristotle criticise this account of the human good on a number of grounds. They think the account of human flourishing too thin. They object to the interpretation of justice offered and would give additional importance to other virtues. They regard the theory as clashing too seriously with pre-theroretical moral opinions. Corresponding things would be said about and against contemporary consequentialist theories. Aretaic theory suggests a method for the proper justification of such theories. It would consist in appeal to: a given conception of the good life, buttressed by moral experience and independently plausible accounts of human powers of action, feeling and intellect. It could not consist in appeal to the form or essence of morality.

One of the major reasons why contemporary aretaic theorists who follow Aristotle reject deontological and utilitarian theories is that they tend to rest upon external epistemologies which are implausible when brought to bear on ethics and which result in accounts of the human virtues (though they are not represented as that) which are much too thin and simplistic. The crux of this criticism takes us back to the practicality of ethics and suggests that among the matters needing to be settled in a final adjudication is that of the relation between the human mind and (practical) reality. D. S. Hutchinson expresses this point very well.

> Much modern moral philosophy seems to start from an . . . assumption, that what matters for us is to have the correct beliefs about ethical questions. Since our circumstances vary in a complex way, it would be very laborious for such a theorist to tell us all the beliefs which we ought to have in all our various circumstances, and in this predicament the theorist often refers to more general principles. Two termini of this process of abstraction are utilitarianism, with its absolutely general injunction, and Kantianism, with its purely formal injunction. And other varieties of moral theory share this (ultimately Platonic) assumption that what we need to live properly is *knowledge* about practical matters. (Hutchinson 1986:2)

Aretaic theory rejects this Platonic assumption, hence its stress on virtues, habits of choice, as the key to ethics.

The arguments of the first three chapters of this book are meant to provide an outline of aspects of moral epistemology which contribute to working out which accounts of the good for human beings are plausible.

Let us note finally in this section that aretaic theory can provide reason for accepting both appeal to act types and rules, on the one hand, and the results of action, on the other, as morally relevant. It is quite within the scope of an aretaic theory to accept that some acts are of their kind praiseworthy, while others are the opposite. For example it may be part of the good life that honouring the demands of friendship is good, while disobeying them is inherently wrong. One aspect of virtue and practical wisdom will be to have a care, so far as is possible, to the consequences that will flow from our actions. If aretaic theory gives prominence to motive in the determination of an act's rightness it is only to motive understood in a special sense, which can include concern for other aspects of action. What matters is motive as the general conception of the good that someone manifests in action and thus the general form of life that an action coheres with.

REASON AND THE HUMAN GOOD

Aretaic conceptions of ethics allow 'top-down' reasoning from general conceptions of human nature back to accounts of the good and happy life, the virtues and to choiceworthy action. One of the most famous features of Aristotle's use of such reasoning is his argument that, whatever the good life is, it is one that displays most fully the exercise of rationality. This argument proceeds on the principle that the worthwhile, praiseworthy life for the human being will be one that allows for the fulfilment of human nature. We can discover what that human nature is by reflecting on the distinguishing *ergon* (translated frequently as 'function') of humanity. That *ergon* is rationality, so the good life is a rational life.

> to say that happiness is the chief good seems a platitude, and a clearer account of what it is still desired. This might perhaps be given, if we could first ascertain the function of man. For just as for a flute-player, a sculptor, or any artist, and in general, for all things that have a function or activity, the good and the 'well' is thought to reside in the function, so it would seem to be for man. (Aristotle 1925a:1097b)

This apparent deduction of the rational life as the summit of the virtues is apt to seem too quick to many critics. First it is not at all clear that humanity has a function. Does this not imply that human nature is analogous to a designed thing, such as a tool? Second it is not apparent that the truly human is found in what distinguishes us from all other things. Why in giving an account of the parts of human nature relevant to ethical reflection should we not equally stress those aspects of our being we have *in common* with other creatures? Third it is not evident that the fully or distinctively human lies in the rational life. There are many things that human beings do that are distinctive of them as a species. Some of them are not very pleasant. Why should these not be morally decisive if Aristotle's basic approach is correct? Finally Aristotle appears to have cut out appeals to other, 'external' ideas about the good life by providing a philosophical deduction of its character. Surely there are metaphysical views which stress quite different aspects of the human than rationality. The critic will see the errors of the argument summed up in the contentions of the final book of the *Nicomachean Ethics* that a life lived in the exercise of philosophical wisdom and contemplation is the most praiseworthy (Aristotle 1925a: 1178ªff). This conclusion seems to seal the narrow intellectualism to which this form of reasoning about the nature of the human good appears bound to lead.

All of these criticisms can be answered. Let us begin by noting that by the *ergon* of humanity Aristotle does not mean to imply that human beings have been designed for a particular purpose. He intends to place consideration of human nature within a general outlook which regards each kind of thing as distinguished by a characteristic mode of activity, a specific way of being and behaving. Excellence for any thing is then a matter of its fulfilling or displaying this characteristic nature. As he says in the *Eudemian Ethics*, excellence lies in a thing's work or employment; living well and doing well for human beings is a mode of activity or employment (1925b:1219ª/ᵇ and compare Hutchinson 1986:22–24). In deciding what is the characteristic mode of being and activity of human beings we need not deny that there will be relationships and overlaps between this and that of other creatures. For example, human beings are like other animals in respect of having sensations. But if we are to discover in what human excellence and perfection might consist in it seems inevitable to seek out those modes of being which are distinctively human. It would be odd, acting on the assumption that there is a distinct mode of excellence or praiseworthiness that is human, to seek its ground in the perfection of attributes which humankind shares with other creatures. And we do assume that in raising the matter of the fundamentals of ethics that there is a distinct set of questions about good and bad in human conduct and character, and thus that there is a distinct way of manifesting *human excellence*.

The very context in which the question as to the foundations of ethics is raised provides an answer to the question of why rationality should be selected as the characteristic basis of human excellence. We engage in ethical reflection when we ask the questions 'What shall we do, how shall we live?' and when we search out the fundamental considerations on which answers to these questions must rest. In this we acknowledge that what is distinctive of human action is that it is answerable to reason. What distinguishes a human act from mere reflex or habitual behaviour or bodily movement (all of which can be displayed by non-human creatures) is that it embodies intention. To say that it embodies intention is to say that a certain type of why-question is appropriate to it, namely the question 'For what reason did the agent act thus?'. The fact that human beings possess a rational soul among other principles of life, says Aristotle, means that they are the source of a special kind of movement. Only they can be said to 'act' (1925b:1219^b and 1220^b). Thus the characteristic mode of human activity consists in the embodiment of reason in conduct and it is this that is the basis of ethical reflection. Excellence in the embodiment of reason in conduct will be the characteristic human good (Hutchinson 1986:59). Stressing the role of reason in human excellence should not be taken to exclude the display of other powers, such as the manifestation of artistic imagination, or emotion. For these will be manifestations of excellence when done in the right way and toward the right things, when, that is, they are infused by a rationally grounded sense of the appropriate and inappropriate. They are excellences only in issuing in praiseworthy forms of *human act*. Rationality in action is thus not an alternative to other ways of being human, but is manifested in them. Displaying reason in conduct thus points to a formal and generic account of human excellence, rather than a concrete and specific way of living well. As such it leaves room for different accounts of human nature to fill out what a life showing reason embodied in conduct will come to. In this respect the funadamentals of an aretaic theory do not entail that intellectualism is the best. Aretaic theorists will set aside, as tangential and secondary, Aristotle's claims in Book 10 of the *Nicomachean Ethics* that a life of philosophical contemplation was the highest. The apparent conclusion there that human excellence is best displayed by the philosopher living on a moderate income is thus dismissed. (Would that it were true!)

Because the claims about human nature, excellence and rationality are formal and generic, aretaic theory offers no *a priori* deduction of a specific way of living that is right for human beings. While this allows differing metaphysical visions to feed in their beliefs about human life and circumstances to the deliberations of moral reason, it also re-confirms the 'bottom-up' nature of much actual moral reflection. The aretaic theorist can accept what was affirmed in the earlier chapters of this study about how conscience has sources in the very structures of the human world and human relationships. However, despite the limitations on deduction of moral principles from theory built into the aretaic account, it does provide some thoughts about the essentials of the human virtues and in this way points to common perceptions about the human good which any metaphysic or world-view will have to take account of.

We can see where these thoughts about the essentials of the virtues might come from by considering what the aretaic theorist says about the emotions.

It is characteristic of the life of human beings as active creatures that much of their responses to circumstances and many of their actions are influenced by feelings. Feelings embody primitive evaluations of features of our circumstances: emotions of love, kindness, anger, fear and the like are unintelligible without their connections to the perception of various forms of value, negative or positive, in their objects. Human emotions provide ways in which we register and perceive value in the world around us. A rational and reflective life contains a movement to questioning and guiding the feelings with which we respond to circumstance. Such questioning and guiding will we possible through rational reflection on the real character of the objects of the emotions and the appropriateness of the value judgements we implicitly make about those objects. It would seem vital then to an examined life which displays rational activity to seek to integrate to the highest possible degree rational reflection on the real worth of the objects around us and our emotions of attraction and aversion to those objects. Consider the alternatives to seeking such integration.

Noting that feelings provide primitive, unreflective judgements of value someone might contend that a truly good life, embodying reason to the highest degree, will be one in which all such emotions are suppressed and stilled. Reason as cool reflection is then the only source of perception and response of value. Considerable psychic conflict may be expected in any attempt to meet this ideal. This hardly suggests a path to human flourishing. Moreover even if such a state could be achieved the resources of excellent activity would have been seriously reduced. Emotions, properly trained, are important ways of perceiving the morally relevant features of our world and of engaging the will in action in the cause of right. The person who is incapable of feeling anger and outrage at injustice and pleasure at the sight and thought of justice displayed lacks an important source of insight and stimulus that the truly just individual has. We can imagine folk who do kind acts merely out of the conscientious reflection that to show consideration for others is correct, but we shall properly place less confidence that they will perceive and act aright in circumstances which demand kindness than in one who who has appropriate kindly feelings. 'For . . . the man who does not rejoice in noble action is not even good; since no one would call a man just who did not enjoy acting justly, nor any man liberal who did not enjoy liberal actions' (Aristotle 1925a:1099a).

If the emotions and their corresponding perceptions of value are not to be stilled can they be ignored in a life worth living? Surely not, for such a life would face conflict at every turn. The range of responses to circumstance provided by the emotions would be in ever present danger of clashing with that which reflection on reasons for action provided. An inconsistency in valuations and a consequent weakening of dispositions to act as we ought can then be expected.

The examined, rational life cannot starve itself of one important source of the perception of value and of action. And it cannot rest content with conflict between sources of these things. The alternative is the closest possible integration between cool reflection upon value and emotional registering of it. It will have to concern itself therefore with the cultivation of some excellences of character which concern the education and training of the emotions in the light of reflection on the appropriateness of the judgements implicit in them. We could equally put this point in reverse: these excellences will concern the infusing of reflective judgements bearing on conduct with the relevant emotions and feelings of pleasure and pain. The ingredients of these human excellences, traits of character, consist in the appropriate integration of desire, feeling and the recognition of reasons for action (Dent 1984:25). This is why Aristotle states that

'We must take as signs of states of character the pleasure or pain that ensues on acts' (1925a:1104^b). He then illustrates this by pointing out how the courageous individual is not simply the one who does the right thing in the face of danger, but he or she who does so with the right kind of spirit. He concludes, 'Hence we ought to have been brought up in a particular way from our very youth . . . so as both to delight in and to be pained by the things that we ought'.

Such facts about the place of the emotions in the life of human beings suggest a range of human excellences in character traits such as kindness and courage which are chiefly concerned with responses based in feeling to other people and our environment. There are other primitive sources of valuation which the rational life in any form will take account of and which in turn suggest further virtues. We have noted earlier how human appetites prompt action. Though not based on judgements of value they create reasons for pursuing and avoiding objects. So my given taste for beer creates a desire and corresponding reason to seek to get it. Once more a life of *rational* activity has to face questions concerning appropriateness and consistency in the things it pursues and avoids. This suggests in turn the need for a virtue or virtues associated with self-control and self-management in the filling of sense appetites. For reasons connected again with the fundamental nature of this aspect of our lives and with a necessary consistency in the reasons for action we acknowledge it seems right neither to attempt to destroy nor to ignore such sources of pleasure and aversion. In the examined life which displays rational activity to the highest degree control over these desires will have been exercised to an extent which enables them to be pursued in the appropriate degree for the appropriate things, when judged by a reflective awareness of value. The guiding and shaping of appetites this entails is a feature of the normal upbringing of most human beings. (The issues for moral psychology it raises are well discussed in Dent's account of the virtues, 1984: chapters two and five.)

As well as suggesting the range of virtues connected with feeling and appetite on the general grounds outlined above, aretaic theory is committed, given its assumptions and some obvious facts about human life, to a range of virtues connected with social life. Aristotle claims that the good life will be self-sufficient, meaning that nothing needs to be added to it to make it worthy of praise and desirable. But he does not intend self-sufficient to mean that it can be manifested in an isolated individual life.

Now by self-sufficient we do not mean that which is sufficient for a man by himself, for one who lives a solitary life, but also for parents, children, wife, and in general for his friends and fellow citizens, since man is born for citizenship. (1925a:1097ᵇ)

In the *Eudemian Ethics* he states that in contrast to God (who is is own well-being) our welfare consists in a relation to something beyond us and that the goal of the political art is to produce friendship between human beings (1925b:1245ᵇ and 1234ᵇ). The social, relational character of the human good is entailed, among other things by the moral epistemology behind Aristotle's account. Knowledge of how to choose depends on integrating emotional and rational aspects of our natures. It depends on acquiring complex skills in recognition and discrimination. It is quite implausible to suppose that such skills in practical reason could be acquired in any other way than through instruction by those with knowledge and experience. It would also seem to involve upbringing in circumstances which aided one in acquiring, integrating and taking due measure of affections and feelings. This would suggest that it is impossible without the existence and virtues of family life (or something like it). We have noted in chapter two how an essential test of moral discrimination based on non-discursive forms of argument is how far others can be found to see the moral case just as one sees it. In these and other ways exercise and acquisition of practical reason seems to involve dependence on others in childhood and adulthood (compare Sherman 1989:129ff).

Aristotle goes further in declaring that politics is the master science that has the human good as its object (1925a: 1094ᵃ/ᵇ). If we think of the prerequisites for acquiring and exercising practical wisdom and the virtues, we are forced to acknowledge that they are only available in well-ordered communities. There will be certain basic forms of human goodness which are the underpinnings of any attempt to realise the full human good in an individual life. They will include things such as self-respect, freedom in action, knowledge and a minimum material prosperity and health. And we will call a community just in so far as it strives to make possible a common enjoyment of these goods, which will in turn allow individuals to make worthwhile efforts to live the good life. Both an individual's respect for the good in itself and his or her sense of dependence on others to realise these and other prerequisites of the good, will lead to promotion of a sense of justice in his or her life. Justice will then emerge as one of the primary virtues for the individual, as well as the paramount virtue in the community and state.

It would seem then that aretaic theory will have no problems with the arguments of earlier parts of this study that many facets of an indvidual's good will be created in relation with others. Deprived of the goods realisable only with others the individual human being will have precious little left of an an individual plan of life worth pursuing. Aretaic theory can accept the contention of those writers who affirm that an ethics for human beings will be one which explains how the good and the right grow out of relationships (compare Fairweather and McDonald 1984:120). Aristotle's lengthy treatment of friendship in Books VIII and IX of the *Nicomachean Ethics* and Book VII of the *Eudemian Ethics* is testimony to this convergence of views. Moreover it would appear that a virtues account of morality, which stresses the centrality of habits of choice and traits of character, is better able than any ethics which gives primacy to rules or consequences to accommodate the importance but flexibility of the norms which grow out of human relationships. What constitutes such relationships are the several forms of faithfulness and trust involved in being another's colleague, friend, parent, partner and so on. Norms and expectations grow out of these forms of faithfulness and trust. But right acknowledgement of them cannot be reduced to the following of rules, nor can they simply be derived from calculation of consequences according to a standard of good independent of the demands of the relationship in question.

As well as the kinds of moral virtue pointed to in the previous paragraphs aretaic theory is able to offer arguments for the necessary place of certain intellectual virtues in any plausible account of the good life. To acquire and exercise the virtues pointed to requires the possession of abilities in judgement, reason and calculation displayed in practical intelligence.

I have offered a brief sketch of arguments from the very general understanding of reason, virtue and human nature in aretaic theory to its tentative delineation of some virtues which all sane moral visions will recognise. These arguments suggest why, on the aretaic view, there should be both convergence and divergence in pictures of the virtues. When we consider the variety of circumstances in which the pursuit of human flourishing must take place and the variety of interpretations which human customs and world views place on those circumstances we should expect the aretaic conception to allow that there will be different concrete realisations of the human good and that diferent world views will argue about what the final components of the good life consist in. In all this I agree with Stuart Hampshire's summary on divergence and convergence in ethics.

> In fact the historically conditioned moralities do converge upon a common core and are not so diverse as relativists claim. Courage, justice, friendship, the power of thought and the exercise of intelligence, self-control are the disciplines that in the abstract ideal are the essential Aristotelian virtues, although the concrete forms that they take greatly vary in the different socially conditioned moralities. The virtues of splendid aristocratic warriors are not the same as the virtues of a Christian monk; but they are not merely different. Each of the two ways of life demands courage, fairness or justice, loyalty, love and friendship, intelligence and skill, and self-control. (Hampshire 1977:44).

Aretaic theory can reasonably expect there to be much common ground on different accounts of the human virtues between different overall world views, provided it is accepted that human good lies in excellent and praiseworthy activity. Of course, some outlooks, notably some religious ones, do not accept this minimal, common starting point. But then they are likely to quarrel with much that is normally considered central to moral concerns. Aretaic theory is not defeated by there being differences over the full and precise delineation of the human good between different metaphysical outlooks provided that the possibility of rational debate between such outlooks is accepted. Indeed, its emphasis on the 'bottom-up' nature of moral reasoning suggests ways in which such debate may be possible. More will be said about these issues in Chapters 7 and 8.

THE GOOD AND THE GOOD FOR HUMAN BEINGS

We have seen that on an aretaic conception of moral reasoning ethical reflection is unified around a conception of the good life for human beings. Right acts are, ultimately, those that would be chosen by one living a good life. A good life for human beings will be a mode of activity, embodying self-examination and reason to the highest degree. Its basic constituents will be a series of virtues. These will be states of character displaying habits of choice integrating rational reflection, desires and patterns of feeling. Different virtues (ignoring the executive, intellectual virtues) will be distinguished by their objects, as courage is distinguished from kindness by the fact that the former considers dangers and perils while the latter considers the well-being and comfort of others. Consideration in the abstract of the form of the examined life of rational activity and of the kinds of important objects that any human life will have to take into account leads to outline accounts of the virtues and thus of the good life. We have seen that the aretaic account can accept limits to how far this abstract portrayal of the good life can go, for different visions of human nature and circumstances will suggest divergent portrayals of the objects and circumstances of human activity. Moreover it is of the essence of aretaic theory to accept that we shall need to judge in the particular case what, say, the appropriate direction of kindness is as we determine the worth of its object. Such detailed specification of the shape of the virtues cannot be provided by a theory, for it is an outcome of moral experience itself and that experience can only be achieved in the living of the moral life. On the aretaic view this is an unavoidable but wholly expected and welcome limitation on a philosophical theory of ethics.

Earlier chapters have indicated tendencies in modern consequentialist and deontological theories to enforce a sharp separation between private good and public right. The good has a subjective basis in preference satisfaction or the contingent and personal patterns of pleasure. Objectivity for morals is maintained through endeavouring to derive public principles of right out of subjective or personal accounts of the good. Aretaic theory in contrast contends for the closest possible integration between private good and public, objective right. There are public principles of right action because there is objective excellence in personal living. Such excellence is compatible with different concrete attempts to realise the good, reflecting individual talents and interests. But there is a basic pattern or structure to good living which all ought to strive for. Public principles of right are required because forms of human cooperation and a just social order are needed as the background to the realisation of the good life for human beings. Though the good life manifests excellence in accordance with our distinctive nature as human beings it is not naturally achieved, where 'naturally' means non-socially, non-relationally. It is a nature which can only be fulfilled in community.

Theories which depend on a private good versus public right contrast have their own difficulties in showing how moral norms can be recommended to all. They need to construct a bridge accross the gap they themselves have created between the obvious, tautologous interest each has in his or her own good and the interest morality expects them to have in the right. Aretaic theory has its own difficulties in explaining the commendatory, normative force behind moral claims. To say that we ought to be kind is to say that we have good reasons so to be. What might these be on an aretaic and how can it be shown that these reasons have overriding force?

As we saw in Chapter 1, the difficulty all accounts of morality face in showing how universal principles of correctness in conduct might have overriding and ultimate sway in the guidance of action provides one of the basic problems on which moral scepticism builds. The success of the aretaic account as a moral theory should not be judged on whether it can decisively refute moral scepticism, but on whether its answer to the sceptic's challenge is at least as convincing as that of other moral theories.

The Aristotle-inspired moralist will want to say of the good life consisting in rational activity that is is the ideal and norm for judging all conduct. It represents flourishing for a human being in two respects: the perfection of our characteristic nature as human creatures, and the way in which a sustainable happiness can be achieved. Now the critic may concede the first part of the claim about the good life and flourishing. In the abstract the life of the virtues may represent an ideal of human perfection. But to the second part of the claim he may reasonably object that the good life is not guaranteed to bring flourishing as happiness to those who are disposed by interests to this kind of life and offers no prospect of happiness to the many not disposed by prior interests to favour it. Here then are two objections to the union of human perfection and happiness in the idea of flourishing behind the notion of the good life.

There are a number of grounds for contending that, for anyone initially disposed to take an interest in the disciplines involved, the good life as we have defined it yields happiness. It is a life which follows on from and will deepen modes of relationship with others which are part of normal upbringing and social intercourse. Within such relationships many more goods and interests will be possible for an individual than without them. It will be a life marked by integration. First there will integration within specific actions: of desire, feeling and reason. Actions characterised by this integration will have that unimpeded movement from conception to intention to performance characteristic of those that yield pleasure. They will satisfy the various parts of the human psyche involved in action. There is thus some reason to agree with the Aristotelian claim that they will be intrinsically pleasant and satisfying. The second form of integration in the good life will be shown in the harmony in different claims of value acknowledged from within it. In the examined life of rational activity the value judgements prompted by appetite, emotion and reason will cohere. Moreover, the rational life will have thought through the priorities to be given in general to different virtues and the ends of action they prompt. The good life will thus be free of long-term conflicts of purpose and valuation. Such a life would also show an integration of private interest and publicly establishable value. This and the other modes of integration indicate why the one who lives the good life can answer the problem of why his or her projects matter and why the self that has them should be respected. Such a life exhibits in addition an integration of its different phases over time. The self behind this life can answer the question 'Who am I and what links the different parts of my life, past, present and future?' There is in this life some kind of 'stable centre to one's concerns' (Dent 1984:214). The stable centre arises out of the concern of the examined life to establish the enduring and objective value of the objects of those concerns and to establish a due order in their value (compare Dent 1984:213–4).

The good life, however, is still subject to contingency and chance. Though it will have established a due order between the virtues, it may face in a particular case a harsh clash between the claims of justice and friendship. It may suffer hardship and persecution, perhaps because of its virtue. If it takes virtue seriously, it may have to sacrifice itself for the objective goods virtue focuses on, as when the courageous individual lays down his or her life to defeat evil. Happiness then seems to require externals to supplement the good life. Aristotle acknowedges this when he asks 'Why then should we not say that he is happy who is active in accordance with complete virtue and is sufficiently equipped with external goods, not for some chance period but throughout a complete life?' (Aristotle 1925a:1101ᵃ).

Part of the force of the objection that happiness depends on contingent externals must be accepted. If we think of the plan for the life of the virtues as revealed in a scheme of education for a worthwhile life, it would have to include acknowledgement that it relied on a reasonable amount of external good luck to guarantee its subject happiness. It may seem that though any overall scheme for a life of activity must presume that contingencies will not destroy it; happiness even for the good man can be wrecked by externals. But here we need to pause, for one important aspect of a life exhibiting the virtues is that it does in some measure make itself free of external mischance. We have already pointed to sources of happiness that come from within the examined, rational life. These point to Aristotle's conclusion that the virtuous person will find virtuous acts intrinsically pleasurable or satisfying. What the virtuous will come to desire is the activity of virtue in itself. It will be a mark of having a virtue that one chooses to do its corresponding acts for their own sakes. They are chosen for their own sakes when they are chose for the sake of the activity involved in doing them (Hutchinson 1986:101-2). We have seen why the activity involved in doing virtuous acts might be chosen for itself. If it is, it matters less, though it still matters, that the objectives of this activity are actually accomplished. Sherman, following Aristotle, sums up this point in saying that 'justice is fine never simply as a productive capacity . . . but rather as a way of acting or living' (Sherman 1989:115). Here is how the worthwhileness of right action for the virtuous becomes independent of the flow of fortune. Aristotle notes how if externals are our touchstones of happiness, we 'should often call the same man happy and again wretched, making the happy man out to be a "chamelion and insecurely based"'. If we have in mind by happiness a stable state then there is reason to think that the virtuous are more likely to have it: 'Or is this keeping pace with his fortunes quite wrong: Success or failure in life does not depend on these, but human life . . . needs these as mere additions, while virtuous activities or their opposites are what constitute happiness or the reverse' (Aristotle 1925a:1100^b). Thus Aristotle suggests that the superiority of virtue lies in the very fact that it better equips its possessor to cope with mischance and frustration.

The question that needs to be considered is not whether the good life is vulnerable to some degree to misfortune and contingency. For all ways of living are so vulnerable. The vicious person is as likely to find that external factors prevents the realisation of some goals and demands self-sacrifice if others are to be achieved. Only a life lived according to a 'plan' of just focusing attention and desire on what the circumstances of life throw up (a determination to find desirable what ever chance dictated was on offer for possession and attainment) could avoid the possibility of frustration and disappointment. But such a life could hardly be one of agency. It would be content to let chance and circumstance dictate goals and would fail of the most minimal coherence. All lives, then, which have settled goals and set store by some ends face the problems aired in respect of the virtuous life. If the vicious person's plans are as likely to be as frustrated as the good person's does he or she have the resources to find the *endeavour* to honour and pursue those plans as worthwhile as the good person possesses? This can only be if the activity of engaging in such conduct is worthwhile regardless of whether it accomplishes its objects. It is arguable that it cannot be. Though there are some who enjoy the planning and means involved in attaining evil ends, it seems improbable to suppose that those who are evil could feel that their time and effort in evil was not misspent when they fail to actually attain their evil objects (Sherman 1989:116).

The final point above takes us on to the question of the sense in which the life of the virtues could be said to be good for those who are not already disposed by the pattern of their extant desires to find it rewarding and satisfying. Any answer must draw upon the points already made about why the good life might be good for those who live it and it must contend that those goods are needed for satisfaction in any characteristically human life in any likely circumstances we can imagine. Reminding ourselves of those goods, they include: the widening of interests following on from normatively governed relations with others, integration in the grounds of action and in the values acknowledged in a life, achievement of objective grounds for self-respect and for a sense of stable selfhood, a measure of independence of the vicissitudes of fortune and the cultivation of internal sources of worthwhileness. The aretaic theorist need not claim that any one with any set of interests will automatically find such a life appealing. It may not be plainly irrational, in the sense of inconsistent with one's extant preferences, to refuse to live such a life. But the aretaic theorist could reasonably claim that any form of human life which has confronted the question 'What ought I to do, what shall I be?' will be a life endeavouring to embody rational activity and that any such life will benefit from the goods achievable in the good life. Those who ignore or reject the claims of the good life can thus be said, with reason, to be in ignorance of how they ought to live if they want to live in a worthwhile and satisfying way.

The question 'Does it pay to be good?' is a naive one. Not any and every set of desires that people have will be satisfied by the ideal life for a human being. But the aretaic theory must rest its case for saying that the virtuous life is not only good but also the good for human beings in the claim that essential goods of agency and selfhood are obtainable only through the endeavour to live that life. Some may not appreciate these goods given their present desires. To take an extreme case, the contented, because brain-washed slave will not. But this still leaves room for the thought that to live without these goods is to live in a piteable way, a way which reflection open to the possibility that there are goods independent of satisfying present desire could not support.

7

Morality without Religion

Part of the aim behind my account of moral thought has been to offer an intelligible background against which the issues surrounding the relation between morality and religion can be considered. These issues are often discussed in an adversarial manner. One the one hand, theistic or Christian thinkers will contend that morality without religion is gravely deficient at best, conceptually impossible at worst; on the other hand, atheistic thinkers claim that religion should have no proper influence upon morals and may indeed be its corrupter. Battle is thus joined over the autonomy of ethics: can morality stand without a religious foundation, or is it something that would be corrupted if based on a religious metaphysic? Even superficial acquaintance with the complex issues raised by these questions reveals that this adversarial treatment of them tends to simplify them. However, for purely pedagogic purposes it is useful to follow out the debate between the two sharply opposed opinions. In the course of discussing them we shall see that the truth is more complex than either presents it.

Discussion which starts from these simple views of morality's links with religion reveals the naivety of a picture of morality which protagonists of either extreme position tend to adopt. Morality tends to be thought of as consisting primarily of a set of binding rules. The theistic critic of secular ethics then claims that the certainty or authority of such rules can be guaranteed only if there is a divine legislator behind them. The secular protagonist claims that God can only be related to morality as rule-giver, and as such He would make morality arbitrary or non-universal. Without this picture of morality as a rule-set, the issues become more complex and the need for battle between religon and secularism for the prize of morality becomes less obvious.

Grounds for arguing that morality is impossible without a religious, theistic grounding fall into two rough classes: those raising matters of motivation and those concerned with epistemological-cum-metaphysical issues.

The simplest argument for concluding that an outlook unconvinced of the existence of a deity can provide no firm motivational grounding for morality turns around the idea of rewards and punishments. For if there is no God it is obvious that there can be no guarantee that living a life which respects moral duties will pay, and that living a life of wickedness will not lead to advantage and prosperity. Thus there will be no clear reason why we should pursue virtue and avoid vice. It seems that it was because of such reasoning that atheism was regarded as destructive of citizenship by eighteenth century writers. They thought that it would take away the necessary motivational foundations for respecting obligations of citizenship such as honouring contracts (see Locke 1975:351–3, 682 and 1978:52).

Arguments of this kind are only remotely plausible if we accept a two-tier view of human motives and interests that we have in fact found reason to question throughout this study. It depends on seeing moral considerations as added onto a range of non-moral interests and desires, which thereafter remain unchanged, only restrained, by an awareness of what is good and right. These non-moral desires remain the source of our real motives and it is mere luck if they are not aggressively selfish. The naivety of this picture is manifold. Moral considerations are not a layer of restraint slapped onto full and determinate non-moral interests. Many desires of many people constitutively depend on interests in others arising out of forms of moral relationship. Moral interests shape the desires of the good human being, who thereafter has reason to find activity in accordance with moral reason satisfying and rewarding. To argue that moral considerations can only motivate if guaranteed to harmonise with pre-moral interests is to offer an implausible picture of the relation between morality and human nature, one that seems to rule out the very existence of any one actually possessing the virtues.

A particular naivety lies in the implicit appeal to the rewards of heaven in such reasoning. Whatever concrete shape we give to the idea of eternal life, it can only be a religiously interesting vision if the good it offers or embodies is morally structured. So that, if we do think about the 'pleasures' of heaven, these will have to rise above nursery visions of continuous supplies of milk and honey. Our ideal of eternal life will have to embody an ideal of the completion and perfection of human striving for the best. So the pleasures of heaven will not in fact be pleasant to those whose basic interests remain unaffected by considerations of the good and the right. Even those postponing the integration of virtue and interest until the after-life will have to learn to find virtue and perfection rewarding and worthwhile at some stage.

The religious and moral naivety of such ways of arguing are painful. In my view the more sophisticated Kantian arguments for the conclusion that God is required to give a viable picture of the highest good fare little better. These can be found in the Dialectic of *The Critique of Practical Reason* (Kant 1956:128–30) and have been given a clear, and in many respects definitive, modern gloss by Green (1978, chapter 3).

We have seen in Chapter 4 that Kantian ethics does not derive moral principles from a substantive end for human life. They flow instead from the demands of rational impartiality, encapsulated in the formula of making universal legislation given by the Categorical Imperative. Yet out of this form of morality an end does flow. The ultimate goal of human striving has to be fulfillment of our rational nature. Impartial moral legislation will promote the existence of us all as rational beings because its rules lay down conditions by which the rational pursuit of maximally satisfying our purposes can be secured. These rules harmonise each person's pursuit of the good with that of others'. Kant's argument for the existence of God as a postulate of practical reason allows for a rational but subjective need to lead to belief in God on the assumption that no meataphysical proof or disproof of God is cogent. The rational need turns around what must be assumed to make sense of striving for the goal of perfecting rational personhood.

Fulfilling rational nature means attaining a state of virtue in which the maxims of one's acts always embody respect for the demands of rational impartiality. One's acts will then always be sufficiently motivated by respect for the moral law. But fulfilling rational nature also means attaining happiness, that is maximally satisfying one's desires and realising the particular plan of life that is one's own. If this world is not morally ordered then there is no guarantee that these two aspects of fulfilling rational nature will not come into conflict. Practical reason will thus be at odds with itself. Attaining a will fully in accord with respect for the law will be at the cost of frustration of personal goals and the prospect of happiness. We need the supposition, then, that despite appearances the world is under moral government (that is happiness is proportioned to virtue in the long run) to avoid the conflict in practical reason and the conclusion that perfecting rational nature cannot be a goal after all. The concrete form that this thought about moral government is that of a God who dispenses happiness in accordance with desert.

There are many questions about this form of reasoning. Green himself notes that it falls short of a proof that ethics requires God (Green 1978:72). For some religions suppose, quite coherently on the surface, that there is a supreme moral mechanism in the universe for adjusting happiness to desert that is *impersonal* in nature. Common criticisms of the argument also turn around whether a demand of practical thought could ever produce belief in a matter of fact (see Mackie 1977:228). For our our purposes it is important to stress that the Kantian proof of the inadequacy of any secular morality depends on the same the sharp division between morality and interests as the cruder argument linking God to the idea of rewards and punishments. Even though the Kantian allows for an independent respect for the claims of morality which motivates, he or she still needs the sharp separation between two orders of reason in order to contend that a religious mechanism is required to stitch back together the goods these respective orders fasten upon. This once more gives rise to religiously incredible thoughts about how eternal life might complete the individual good. Is it going to satisfy the good man's private, interest-based good whatever that may have been, even if it consisted in something utterly trifling and silly? It will face all the difficulties rehearsed about keeping the two orders of reason apart in the life of good men and women. The agnostic or atheistic moralist can surely side-step whatever force the argument has by conceding that if the Kantian insists on locating good initially in subjective, interest satisfaction and keeping that notion divorced from moral reason thereafter, he or she *will* have to resort to desperate measures at the end of the day to produce a coherent account of the end of action. The solution is to avoid divorcing these ideas of good in the first place.

Having seen the weakness of the Kantian claim that practical reason contradicts itself if it abandons the idea that the world is under ultimate moral government, it is still possible to claim that a wholly secular ethics leaves the pursuit of the good pointless if it has no answer to the problems raised by human finiteness and the world's evil. As Meynell has claimed of the 'man of good will':

> He must *want* it to be true that in the long run oppressors will not derive advantage from their oppression, that the innocent and righteous will ultimately achieve fulfillment at least approximately in accordance with their virtue. I conclude that the clear sighted man of good will must wish that theism, or at least something with equivalent eschatalogical implications, were true; or at any rate that he cannot regard its falsity as less than a moral tragedy. (Meynell 1972:233)

An argument for the contention that the secular moralist must regard the lack of an ultimate justice as a tragedy can be given along the following lines (from Mitchell 1980:142–3). An important part of moral virtue consists in a principled concern for other's needs. It must follow that the fulfillment of other's needs matters to the virtuous. If their actions are frustrated by the unjust or by mischance and do not actually enhance the fulfillment of others then they are pointless. Moreover, if the meeting of other people's needs matters to the virtuous individual, so must the satisfaction of his or her needs. Hence, the virtuous person cannot claim that his or her own acts retain a moral point (or *all* their moral point) if they don't actually lead to (a) the happiness of others and (b) his or her own happiness. At least some of the point of living a good life will be lost if good actions do not in fact promote others' and one's own happiness. Part of the motive for living that life is taken away unless there can be an assurance that living the good life contributes to the desired effects for others and oneself. Only the existence of a non-human, undefeatable agency for justice which will complete it purposes in some ultimate state can provide this assurance.

These arguments register dissatisfaction with the contentions about the life of virtue and its inherent desirablity offered in the previous chapter. They point to the fact that secular ethics has its own problem of evil, which it must honestly face, just as theistic outlooks must face their problem of evil (compare Kekes 1990:4 and *passim*). Meynell and others fasten upon one notable outcome of evil: the frustration of human needs and purposes, and in particular the needs and purposes of good men and women. The sources of this evil outcome are manifold. They include: the evil characters and skills of bad people, contingencies and chance within the course of nature that limit the success of human endeavours, and the general problems of human finiteness which also poison and frustrate human striving (death, limited knowledge and power and goodness). All these factors entail that the human order, considered without reference to a religiously sanctioned eschaton, always falls short of complete justice. It is part of the aim of justice to make the human world a complete moral order. In a genuinely moral order their would be a harmony between what is deserved by the principles of justice and experienced happiness. Many of our actions show allegiance to the desire to create such an order – as when we reward the deserving and punish the guilty. In one respect at least the secular moralist can accept that religious world views solve this problem, for whatever else may be unclear about them they contain a promise that somehow or other our efforts to create such an order in the face of human weakness and wickedness and the world's apparent indifference will be successfully topped up by a non-human agency.

The religious solution to the problem of the world's injustice is no doubt rejected by many agnostic or atheistic thinkers because the intellectual commitments that any version of it brings are felt to be questionable on other grounds. The question that concerns us is whether the alleged deficiencies in secular ethics are serious enough to provide independent confirmation of the truth of a religious outlook. One issue that needs immediate consideration is the relation between the religious and the secular problem of evil. *Prima facie* there is a difficulty behind the religious moralist laying too much weight on the extent to which human and natural deficiencies entail that this mundane existence is thoroughly unjust. Such a stress gives greater prominence to the question of the motives and power of the divine agency that is, after all, responsible for the existence of the conditions which lead to this unjust order. It also threatens to widen the gulf between morality and its point in this world and the promised fulfillment of human good in the next. That is, it tends to rob human effort in this world of point and produce the morally and religiously unsatisfactory dismissal of this life as rather messy and pointless curtain-raiser to a life beyond.

The counter-difficulties in the religious critique raised so far are no more than warnings of potential flaws. We can develop these points further by considering first the social aspect of morality. One of the important dimensions of morality that contractarian and utilitarian theories usefully bring out is that of a set of rules for the ordering of society and the regulation of interaction between its members. If our religiously inspired picture of the mundane world's injustice is too harsh, it may well lead (as indeed it has in some theologies) to a social and political indifferentism which is deeply unattractive to many. I have in mind views that maintain that since the world is in such a deep mire and cannot be improved by human effort we should not bother trying; we should renounce it. For a variety of reasons religious moralists in the twentieth century wish to claim that human effort to create a just social order is important at the level of more than gesture. It is arguable indeed that morality as a set of rules and principles for the creation of a worthwhile social order is actually given greater rather than less point by reflections on the prevalance of evil. As stressed by some contemporary deontologists and utilitarians, moral rules and their social propagation and enforcement matter precisely because they provide one of the important ways in which human tendencies to evil can be countered. Indeed, in some versions of these theories the major point of morality as the foundation of a social system lies in the way in which its rules serve to mitigate human weaknesses and tendencies to evil (for example Gert 1973, see 157 especially). I think that if we followed these thoughts through in detail we would hardly see the fact of evil and injustice as making morality-without-God pointless. Indeed if we rule out divine ways of combatting human evil, the role of morality as a set of enforceable social rules becomes even more important.

If the case against the point of secular ethics is pressed it looks as if it will have to focus on morality as the guide and goal of personal living. And here, though the religious moralist might concede that secular ethics has a perfectly good answer to the question 'What is the point of there being an institution called "morality"'?, secularism is on much weaker ground with the question 'What is the point in *me* being moral?' (compare Green 1978:13). In other words, the root of the objection to secular ethics is that it can offer the individual who respects morality no guarantee of anything other than a life of disappointment and self-sacrifice.

This question was considered in Chapter 6, where it was argued that there may be point to individual virtuous activity independent to some extent of its outcome (for the virtuous individual's prospering) because there was an inherent value in pursuing the goals and aims of virtue. The goods of virtue were in part the goods of rational activity itself. Now it appears that the religious moralist must accept part of this case. The religious eschaton that completes the good must be one that depends for its realisation on the acquisition of virtue. If not, then the point of virtue is destroyed by the promise that the divine will give one happiness without the effort of becoming virtuous. Moreover being virtuous must be a component part of the final good in the eschaton. It is religiously, psychologically and morally unatisfactory to consider the attainment of virtue as if it were merely passing a winning post, after which one was given a reward wholly unrelated to it. So as an integral component part of the ultimate good (in the theistic traditions typically the vision and perfected love of God) the virtuous life must have some degree of inherent value and worthwhileness. But perhaps, the critic will argue, it is a component part whose worth, while it adds to the whole, essentially depends on its integration with other aspects. So that if being virtuous did not lead to the fulfillment of other worthwhile aspects of the good its point would be lost as well. As Mitchell puts it:

> God's purpose for men would have to be such that it cannot be achieved without the pursuit of moral virtue, but not such that is consists simply in the achievement of moral virtue. He who would save his soul must be willing to lose it, but there must be more to saving one's soul that the willingness to lose it. (Mitchell 1980:143).

This argument acquires force from the point that secular, virtue ethics regards living virtuously as a component of a larger good, to be completed by reasonable material satisfaction and a degree of good fortune. Such surrounding conditions would appear to be required for the good of the exercise of rational activity to be enjoyed fully.

Having admitted that the good life is a union of virtuous activity with some surrounding goods, the secular moralist must concede that secular thought can offer no sure guarantee in the face of the world's contingencies and evils that this complete good is attainable. There are three main points secular ethics can make to mitigate the impact of the doubts about the point of morality these concessions give rise to. One is the insistence that, as argued in Chapter 6, virtuous living remains a partial good even if it exists in isolation from the ideal whole. It is not a good whose worthwhileness depends solely on its place in an admittedly better whole. A second point takes us back to the social dimension of morality. That dimension increases in importance once more, for the best chance of attaining the complete good will be in a morally ordered community where the social effect of well respected moral rules will increase the chances of being able to enjoy the goods of rational living. A third point reminds us that, on the view of morals defended here, concern for moral considerations is not wholly derived from desire to attain an ultimate good. Moral considerations have a deeper hold over us than that. Some of them are constitutive of our being as persons who have a range of interests unintelligible independent of entering into moral relationships.

We can see from this discussion of moral motivation that what is and is not a proper and sufficient motive for moral action is a complex matter – much more complex than neat proofs of the unsatisfactoriness of this or that moral outlook allow. We shall need to recall this point in Chapter 8 when considering arguments for the conclusion that religious accounts of ethics destroy morality. Our discussion of secular ethics and motive seems to highlight two questions for further reflection: 'Must an adequate ethics have an account of an ultimate, complete good?' and 'Must an adequate ethics be able to guarantee that such a good is attainable?'

THE METAPHYSICS AND EPISTEMOLOGY OF
SECULAR ETHICS

The arguments considered in the previous section tried to show that no moral theory can be uncommitted to the existence of God and have a workable account of moral motivation. I now turn to consider the attempt to show that if we are doubtful of the truth and rationality belief in God, we must be doubtful of the truth and rationality of moral principles. There are a number of arguments for this conclusion. They vary from the more general and abstract to the more specific. The former contend that the truth and rationality of morality as a whole would be threatened without a theistic backing. The latter argue for this conclusion in relation to some specific, though important types of moral principle. Since these more specific arguments are easier to follow I shall begin with them.

If we wish to find examples of important moral judgements which can not be justified within a secular ethics, then the most most frequently discussed are judgements to the effect that certain types of action are forbidden come what may. What is allegedly difficult for the secularist to justify is the idea that a rule, such as 'Do not murder' should be followed regardless of its consequences. Thus the secular moralist is faced with two choices: either he or she relies on mere intuition for the feeling that some acts are not to be done no matter what the consequences, or he or she reasons in the fashion of the consequentialist and accepts that nothing is so bad that it cannot be well done in some circumstances. It is on the basis of this type of argument that Mitchell alleges that in the twentieth century the 'traditional conscience' is faced with painful dilemmas created by its abandonment of Christian beliefs, on the one hand, coupled with its continued commitment to a morality of principle rather than expediency, on the other (Mitchell 1980:91–2).

A good deal lies behind this alleged problem of justification. Sometimes it is the thought that the only resources a secular moralist can draw upon in reasoning about conduct is the calculation of the good states of affairs that will result from action and that such calculation leaves us with no principled, firm moral prohibitions. We have seen reason in earlier chapters to doubt all of this. Even consequentialist thinkers, if they are indirect utilitarians, will try to take seriously the idea that in real life it is worth while sticking fairly rigidly to some basic moral rules, while there are a variety of secular moral theories which have more complex accounts of the relation between right acts and good consequences. Our own favoured aretaic theory admits goodness and badness, right and wrong, in the structure of moral relationships and it can see them embodied in acts themselves (arising out of their relationship to habits of choice in a life as a whole). Matters are worse if we adhere to the 'religious' justification of absolute prohibitions made popular by Peter Geach (Geach 1969:129). In this the decisive factor which stops us doing an act generally thought evil but in a given case productive of good consequences is the fact that to do so would entail violation of divine command, for we cannot balance the attainment of future goods against the cost of disobeying God (since God is the source of the providential order which we think will lead to those goods). Van den Beld comments on this 'Therefore, as far as the believing Christian is concerned, the causal prospects of his or her alternative courses of action cease to matter at precisely the point at which an action commanded or forbidden by God is involved' (van den Beld 1988:115). This kind of justification of principled action brings with it all the faults of simple divine command theory (to be aired more fully in the next chapter). If there is nothing in the act itself or its immediate circumstances that makes it wrong, and if it will produce more overall future good than harm, we must ask why would a divine command continue to forbid it or refuse human beings the right in this case to break a previously firm moral rule? The divine command appears utterly arbitrary and therefore does not provide us with a good moral reason for obeying it in this case. Alternatively, if there is something wrong with our putative evil act and God forbids it because of that, then it is not to be done even if one does not recognise the existence of divine commands.

If consequentialist reasoning and reflection on divine commands are the only sources of moral thought, we might indeed have difficulty justifying the idea of principled prohibitions upon conduct. But we all have to hope, regardless of our religious affiliations, that there are more resources for reason in ethics than these.

Mitchell's dilemma for the traditional conscience appears to be more firmly based and begins from the example of the sanctity of life. Except perhaps in the most extreme and unusual circumstances we acknowledge a bar upon killing the innocent. We thus recognise a value in human life that cannot be reduced to its leading to greater pleasure over pain or to its utility for others. In fact we will have to defend it on the basis of a metaphysic, some large-scale description of what human life is and how it relates to the natural world. This is what a Christian metaphysics can do. It relates the value of each life to a divine creation of it and a divine concern for its ultimate fulfillment. Without a corresponding metaphysic the secularist's concern for the value of life will remain based upon unsupported intuition. It is difficult to see how a naturalist metaphysics could yield the necessary strong prohibition on killing (see Mitchell 1980:74–78).

We shall assume that this kind of argument can be generalised to cover other kinds of deep prohibitions (such as those against torture, human slavery, judicial punishment of the innocent – many of them do seem to be connected with the value of life in so far as they touch upon respect for persons). What might the argument prove? One thing that it does indicate is in harmony with the general argument of this book. It implies that a complete ethics needs a substantive account of the human good and thus some connections with general thoughts about human nature. This does establish the potential relevance of religious world-views to ethical enquiry. This is a theme which will be taken up in Chapter 8. We have seen that in contrast contemporary consequentialist and deontological outlooks tend to opt for very thin accounts of the good and derive the substance of their theories from accounts of the form of morality or the procedures of moral reason. It may be that these outlooks will have difficulty with traditional prohibitions which protect life and the person. (This last point is arguable.) Mitchell alleges that secular outlooks in the contemporary world will be driven, without a metaphysical basis, to regard moral demands as the outcome of personal or social choice and that will be incompatible with giving them a categorical basis. What seems to be in question here is whether a non-religious description of human nature and of a substantive, full human good can be offered. This would be the kind of account of the good which entailed that it does not depend upon choice for its existence, so that even if someone chose to live a life of voluntary slavery because that was what his or her preferences demanded, we would still have room to argue such a life was wrong. At this point we return to familiar territory, namely the question of giving a rich account of the human good based upon the idea that there are goods and harms independent of preference. If the argument of this book is correct then this can be done without appeal to religious premises. This is exactly what Chapter 6 tries to do. Granted that we leave preference-based accounts of the good behind, then it is possible to argue that rational nature in human persons is to be respected regardless of its social utility or the state of the personal preferences of individuals who have that nature. From this we might move to a respect for persons morality which is not subject to the easy exceptions which Mitchell rejects. We do not need to suppose that life or liberty are valuable only because personal or social choice make them so.

Only by first thinning out the options available to secular morality can its religious critic prove that it cannot justify principled stands against expediency in ethics. A similar process can perhaps be seen in attempts to argue for more general metaphysical and epistemological deficiencies in secular ethics. One such attempt arises out of the arguments of John Mackie's *Ethics: Inventing Right and Wrong*.

Mackie favours the preference-view of value alluded to frequently in this study. It follows from this view that the principles of ethics are not true or false in virtue of the nature of any reality independent of human choice. He endorses an account of morality which is roughly similar to that of Gauthier: moral values are the outcome of collective choice. This position can appear to give morality as social rules a measure of objectivity provided that the rational constraints on the collective choice of social rules are stressed. But Mackie's most striking rhetoric in describing morality is sceptical and subjectivist in tone. Following his book's title it stresses the extent to which human attitudes are the source of value and to which ordinary thought is misled by supposing that statements about the right and the good report qualities in reality. Hence, as we saw in Chapter 1 the view that value is created by human choice and preference can lead to a striking account of moral scepticism. Mackie is not disturbed by this reading of his basic case, regarding the discovery that morality is there to be invented by collective choice more liberating than threatening. However, he gives ammunition to religious critics of secular ethics by contending that the only alternative to the preference/choice view of value, and thus the only bulwark against a version of moral scepticism, is one that gives humanity a divinely instituted purpose. Mackie's argument on this score contains both an acknowledgement of the power of aretaic moral theory and a criticism of its basis. If we could make sense of the idea that there was a good for each and everyone that grew out of the characteristic nature of the species, then we might have a value independent of choice. However, the only way to accept that the idea of human nature has the power to delimit a common good for us all independent of preference is through the further thought that there is a divinely instituted purpose behind human nature which will determine that, regardless of individual choice, our good will lie in certain prescribed directions (Mackie 1977:230–232).

Mackie's case appears to take the *ergon* argument of Aristotle as showing that only if human nature has a characteristic function will it have a characteristic good, and it will only have this function if there is a non-human purpose which lays down that such-and-such modes of living will be found ultimately satisfying by us all (and which then shapes the world accordingly). Thus and only thus are individual preferences for the good trumped. No wonder then that Mackie, being sceptical of religious belief, sticks with his subjectivist picture of value, and that religious moralists welcome his case as proving that only a religious metaphysic of morals saves us from the horrors of moral scepticism (Mitchell 1980:155). One who accepts Mackie's view of value could of course endeavour to escape the implication that it implies a kind of moral scepticism by stressing allegedly narrow constraints from the nature of rationality or from the essence of morality on the collective choice of rules. However, we have criticised Mackie's argument in advance, and hence already commented on its limited options for secular ethics, by offering an alternative reading of the *ergon* argument in Chapter 6 and by pointing at a number of places to the inherent implausibility in the preference/choice view of value. If there is a characteristic good for human beings merely because there is a characteristic form of activity that is human, and if the basic notion of good we need in ethics is one of a value that is graspable by reason and in need of objective confirmation, then the force of Mackie's points can be escaped. We have at least presented aretaic ethics in Chapter 6 in a manner which does not make it immediately dependent on a doctrine of creation.

We must note as important, and deserving of consideration, the perceptions shared by a number of authors that underly this particular type of critique of secular ethics. First we have the thought (we which we have in part supported) that aretaic ethics provides the only sure remedy against forms of moral scepticism. Second we have the thought shared by some secular and some religious thinkers that aretaic ethics only makes sense when supported by a doctrine of creation and of divine purposes for humanity.

A general critique of secular ethics would be most convincing if it could show that moral scepticism of the kind outlined in Chapter 1 above was only answerable on the basis of theistic assumptions. Such a critique faces one of the major problems we pointed to in moral scepticism of any kind. It will have to show that there is something especially problematic about *moral thought* on secular premises. It is relatively straightforward to make a case against secular ethics appear powerful if it is part of a general case that notions of truth and reason *simpliciter* are problematic without the support of a theistic metaphysics. A general critique of this kind focusing on the problem of knowledge in a secular world view is illustrated in the Devine's *Relativism, Nihilism, and God* (1989:77–92). If secular thought is denied any viable notions of reason and truth, then it is of course easy to show that it has no workable moral philosophy. Devine's specific arguments against the possibility of notions of reason and truth in secular *ethics* are comparatively sketchy and contain no real acknowledgement of the variety and depth of secular theories of ethics, be they utilitarian, deontological or aretaic.

If the secular theorist is allowed use of the notions of truth and reason in general, then only demonstrations that *ethics* needs a developed theoretical basis to be epistemically acceptable, and that no secular theory works, can show that secular ethics is epistemically unsound. Let it be noted that if there is viable notion of reason in secular ethics then metaphysical problems about the source and nature of value appear to dissolve. Thus worries of the kind 'But where do moral standards come from on a secular view?' cease to be of great interest. There is no need to go through a list of possible sources (such as: personal choice, social custom, evolution). So long as the secular thinker can point to good reasons which back a judgement such as 'Do not steal', the question of whence this moral standard arises is of no more philosophical interest than the question 'Where do the principles of arithmetic come from?' There can be genuine enquiries in psychological and sociological science into how flesh and blood people acquire their moral standards. But so long as some standards are backed by genuine reasons then these causal enquiries are not going to undermine secular ethics.

Appeal to the notion of reason also suggests that the secularist faces no insuperable problem when faced with the metaphysical question of what exactly values are and how they get into the world. For to say that there are real moral values is to say no more than that there are genuine reasons for guiding human conduct and thinking some acts choiceworthy and others not. A frequently cited criterion of the real in philosophy is this: what is real is what has explanatory power. So we say unicorns are merely fictional because nothing that happens in world demands the truth of statements asserting the existence of unicorns in order to be accounted for. To say that moral values are real will be to say that some things cannot be explained without the assumption that some acts and some connected states of affairs are genuinely good or bad independently of people's opinions about whether they are good or bad. Now the things that can only be explained properly by this assumption of value independent of opinion may indeed be things in the human world. These will include the convergence of moral opinion after proper argument on the nature of human choices. But this fact does not establish that the relevant values are unreal (in the sense of being created by human decision, choice or preference; Wiggins 1991 has a fuller argument for my conclusion). Moral values may have an existence which is relative to a human context, in particular the context of choice, reasoning about conduct and the flourishing of human nature. But it does not follow that they are unreal, even if we can agree that without human beings as rational creatures they would have no actual (as opposed to potential) existence.

One final point about the epistemology and metaphysics of morals needs to be made that will serve as a link with the next chapter. We cannot consider how secular ethics might be deficient from a religious standpoint without thinking how religion allegedly solves these deficiencies. On a simple view of religion's remedies for deficiencies in secular thought (and many such views are simple) it is the idea of divine will that solves the problems raised. The discovery and authority of the divine will gives certainty in ethics independent of the vicissitudes of human opinion and culture. The divine will brings values and standards into being. Both diagnosed deficiency and remedy ignore the possibility that there can be no simple escape from the relativity and uncertainty of human opinion or easy answer to the question of the metaphysical status of value. Opinions about the direction and interpretation of the divine will are subject to as much dispute and cultural variation as are found in moral thought – not surprisingly, since moral thought is one means for interpreting and supporting the claims of religion. If we worry that, in contrast to the hard, clear-cut realities described by science, values appear subjective and arbitrary it will hardly comfort us to know that they are founded on divine decrees. We appear to swap one subjectivity and arbitrariness for another.

In conclusion we may suggest that is a dangerous path for a religious outlook to weaken the secular basis of ethics. A viable religious ethic may need to root morality in human judgement and the human world if it is to play its proper role in the economy of human, religious nature. But that very rooting will allow for the existence of resources for moral reason independent of explicit religious backing.

8

Morality with Religion

Arguments against the possibility of religion serving as a foundation of, or influence upon, morality usually begin by criticising the most extreme version of the thesis that morality flows from religion. Once this argumentative target has been destroyed it is hoped that the full autonomy of ethics can be established. Though this strategy has disadvantages apparent at first glance, it is worth following its twists and turns, for it has influenced much philosophical debate and can be used as an introduction to the issues.

The extreme thesis under initial attack by secular critics of theological ethics offers an account of morality as consisting in a set of moral rules which flow from divine commands. The divine will is the necessary and sufficient source of the truth and authority of moral rules. Theological ethics is thus connected with what has come to be known as the simple divine command theory of moral requirements. The theory appears to be asserting that basic moral notions such as right and wrong can be defined in terms of theological ones, specifically in terms of what is prescribed and proscribed by divine will.

Simple divine command theory is thought to be refuted by appeal to the Euthyphro dilemma. This offers the theorist a choice. Either: what is right is so simply because God commands it; or: God commands what is right because it is right. The first horn accepts the terms of the divine command theory but hints at the problems these generate. If what is right is so simply because of the direction of God's command, then independent of those commands there is no distinction between right and wrong. So God could have had no moral reasons for prescribing acts of benevolence and proscribing rape. Equally, we can have no moral reason for obeying God's commands. Without a knowledge of divine commands no one may know of the distinction between right and wrong. These consequences seem threatening to the foundations of morality but the second horn of the dilemma is held to be equally unwelcome. For if God commands what is right because it is right, then the divine will must conform to independent rules of right. There is a distinction between right and wrong independent of divine commands. This appears both to make divine commands irrelevant to ethics and to set limits to divine omnipotence and creation, for morality far from being created by divine will, is independent of that will and conditions it.

The force of the dilemma can be better appreciated by considering a distinction between types of properties that emerges in Plato's discussion which gives the Euthyphro dilemma its name. Plato is concerned with the question how to define righteousness or piety. He considers the definition that righteousness is by definition 'what is loved by the gods'. If that is how to define 'piety' then something follows about the nature of the property it refers to. It must be like the properties of being seen, led, produced, carried (Plato 1963:178,10b). Things have these properties only in virtue of the action of something else upon them. They are extrinsic, not part of their natures. If 'being right' *means* 'being commanded by God' then rightness is such an extrinsic property. As an extrinsic property, rightness fails to have any explanatory power and can be affixed to or detached from actions regardless of their intrinsic natures. So referring to an acts rightness has no power to account for why God prescribes it. Had He chosen to prescribe completely different acts then they would have been right. Being an extrinsic property, rightness does not connect with the nature of acts of courage, generosity or justice, nor is it incompatible with the nature of acts of cowardice, meanness or injustice. If, however, we conclude that rightness, goodness and the like are intrinsic properties of acts, then they acquire explanatory power, become connected with the nature of the acts they qualify, but all at the cost of being properties which acts would have independently of the direction of the divine will.

There is a defeasible presumption that any account of the foundations of morality should respect the standard, defining features of morality, particularly its rationality, authority and universality. *Prima facie* the simple divine command theory, as embodied in the first horn of the Euthyphro dilemma, does not do this. The rationality of ethics is called into question, because it looks as if there are no morally relevant reasons which might guide the divine will one way or the other in laying down moral rules, and no way in which human creatures could fathom what the direction of divine will might be in advance of being instructed in it. These consequences follow from the fact that it is divine prescriptions and proscriptions that create the morally relevant reasons on which ethical judgement is based. The authority of moral rules is called into question because we could not give those rules the respect demanded of things backed by the highest claims of reason. We would have no reason for obeying God's commands other than fear (for we could not obey Him because we knew His commands were independently right). We would know that His commands could have been different and thus are in a real sense arbitrary. The universality of moral rules is threatened if we accept the natural corollary of the simple divine command theory that those who do not know of the express will of God have no knowledge of the basis of right and wrong. Morality would on the surface be reduced to the rules of an exclusive group, those who happened to be aware of the contents of true revelation.

It is not surprising in the light of the above points to find authors (Nowell-Smith 1966, Rachels 1981) claiming that religious ethics and divine command theory violate the autonomy of moral agents. In Chapter 2 we argued that this autonomy is founded on the fact that possession of the mental and emotional capacities of a normal human being is enough to give someone the capacity to make moral judgements. No extra faculties or esoteric sources of knowledge are required. Simple divine command theory suggests the opposite. It also suggests that where individuals have the capacity to make moral judgements they should not exercise it but should be willing to accept as right whatever is commanded by God, regardless of what their consciences declare to be acceptable.

Behind standard criticisms of divine command theory lies the thought that theological judgements – be they be about the direction of divine commands or anything else – can only be of relevance to morality if moral principles antecedent to those judgements are brought to bear upon them. This is the reasoning implicit in the claim that a divine command can be the foundation of a moral rule only if there is genuine moral reason independent of divine commands for obeying God's commands. Sometimes this general thought is framed in terms of the fact/value distinction (see Chapter 1 above). Since, allegedly, no judgement of value follows from factual premises alone, arguments from the fact that God commands such-and-such will always have a suppressed premise to the effect that we ought to obey God. But such a premise is a substantive judgement of value, so there must be a substantive set of moral reasons which lie behind it (compare Frankena 1981:18–19). I leave aside the question of whether the fact/value distinction is of vital relevance in this debate. It does appear that, on any view, we have good reason to assert that prior to bringing in God as the foundation of morality some account must be offered to suggest why the human relationship with the divine is of moral significance. This appears to entail that some moral considerations must be initially independent of religion, at least in this sense: they can be appealed to justify the moral relevance of any religious claims deemed to be important in morality. Whether this basic point also entails that *ultimately* all or the most important moral considerations are independent of religion is another matter. The secular critic takes the failure of the extreme account of morality's dependence on religion to betoken the failure of any account of that dependence. Is he right in this?

If we reflect on the bearing of religion upon morality in the context of theistic forms of faith, then it appears central to consider what the relevance to ethics might be of the human relationship with a personal deity. Hence it is no mere aberration that the notion of divine commands figures so prominently in these discussions. *One* important way in which we might be related to a personal deity is as subjects to a source of legislation. Discussion of human analogies to this relationship might help us better determine its possibilities and limitations.

Consider the relationship between citizen and state. Political philosophers invariably agree that neither a normative nor a descriptive account of the state can work unless it acknowledges that the citizen's relation to the state creates an obligation in him or her to obey the state's laws. The control that the state does and ought to exercise over citizens requires more than mere force on the state's part and fear on the citizens' if it is to be explained. Citizens have an obligation to obey the state's authority. This indeed is what makes the power that the state exercises into authority and not mere might. Authority is power plus perceived legitimacy, power plus the right to be obeyed. Authority is in turn unintelligible unless there is some moral context behind the formation and enforcement of the state's laws and directives. There must be goods and rights independent of the content of particular systems of state authority. These goods must be fostered and respected by a state and its laws to make it worthy of obedience by its citizens. Such goods would include justice, internal and external security and a measure of freedom. The conditions for power in the state to become legitimate entail that enactment by the state does not make a thing right, in the absence of background conditions, and also that what is commanded by the state does not exhaust all that is right. But note that these facts do not entail that the laws of the state do not add to what we are obliged to do. It would be odd indeed to argue that, because there are background conditions of a moral kind to the creation of authority in, and obligation to, the state, so there was no such thing as distinct obligation to the state at all. The citizen who lives under legitimate power and genuine authority will rightly feel that much of what he or she regards himself or herself as obliged to do depends on the content of the state's laws.

So far we have recalled the outlines of extrinsic theories of political obligation, justifying the state's right to command by reference to things which are good independently of those commands. The insights of organic theories of political obligation will help us develop a richer analogy for the relation between religion and morality. Organic theories tell us that the obligation to obey the state emerges out of the identity between state and citizen when state power is legitimate. This identity is founded upon the relationship between the goods recognized by the individual and those made possible by citizenship. It would be a mistake to suppose that authority is granted to the state solely because individuals can perceive a range of ends which they cannot achieve without a measure of obedience. Many of the goods in an individual life will be established as goods only in consequence of education in citizenship. Some of them will be goods of citizenship in all circumstances. There are goods arising out of forms of social living and social cooperation only possible if one lives in some mature, well-ordered community or other. Other individual goods are intelligible only as the product of living in a particular organized society, arising out of the way its mores and customs create the possibility of and encourage certain aspirations. Legitimate government is in accordance with the customs and forms of social life of the community and these in turn shape individual aspirations. Hence we have a kind of identity between state and citizen and the state is rightly obeyed.

Aquinas appears to have had analogies between the moral obligations created in directing a human community and those created by the creative will of God in mind when he gave a common definition of 'law' to cover its use in talking of human laws and the divine laws that are the foundations of morality: 'Law is nought else than an ordinance of reason for the common good made by the authority of who has care of the community and promulgated' (Aquinas 1966b:17). The key terms 'authority', 'reason' and 'common good' indicate that the eternal law which is the foundation of the natural, moral law is surrounded by a moral context. It is with reason that God establishes the conditions that we must follow in the proper direction of our lives and these conditions are related to the achievement of the human good. So not any old commands by any being with omnipotence will have the authority of moral law. Authority in the divine decrees that are the source of the moral law depends on a goodness and respect for moral requirements in God that are independent of the precise content of those decrees.

In the case of the human political order we acknowledge that, though there are considerations of right and wrong separate from the content of law, the direction of sovereign authority creates obligations that did not exist prior to its decrees. This is so because we recognize a general reason for having some sovereign authority and specific reasons for obeying this one. We discern that many aspects of our own individual goods cannot be achieved unless that authority is maintained and supported. Similar, corresponding points apply to the divine–human case. Though not any omnipotent being would be the source of moral law, we recognize that one who is rightly called 'Lord' is worthy of obedience, and thus that His will creates obligations in us.

Unless we recall all the implications of the nature of law, the political analogy which we have had recourse to may suggest an external relationship between divine will and human judgement. Divine will is met as a series of commands which we, with good reason, obey. However, there is an internal and external aspect to law. In the political case this is shown in the way that law, where successful, creates an order in human society, following but also moulding and directing the way of life proper to that society. In this respect citizens obey law in following and taking for granted the order that it creates in their daily transactions (Lucas 1980:100). Law is not then external command backed by sanction. The existence of an internal dimension to law is even more true in the case of God's deliverance of the moral law. For while human law only creates an order in society fallibly and indirectly, eternal law is perfectly and directly creative. Aquinas asserts that the natural moral law, deriving from the eternal law, is within us, both through the structure of our natural aptitudes and through our possession of reason which enables us to discern for ourselves the good it lays down (Aquinas 1966b:23). God's law creates an order in human nature and the world which determines what human flourishing and the good shall consist in. His will can thus be discerned not merely or primarily as external commands but also and largely in the rational discovery of the rules and principles which must be followed if the human good is to be attained. It is the fact that divine will is infallibly and directly creative in establishing an order in human nature and human circumstances which makes the religious problem of evil such a profound one. That is to say, there is created a forceful and nagging demand to explain how the perceived order in creation differs from that which should follow from its embodying divine will.

Simple divine command theory is open to easy refutation because it deprives reference to relationship with God of any of the moral and epistemological background which might make that reference explanatory of the structure and content of ethics. With the appropriate background we can see how it can be argued that, if there is a God, our relationship to Him, can be regarded as the foundation of ethics. It will be such because: (a) His express commands will be a unique source of moral obligation; (b) His will in creation will be the ground of the nature of human flourishing and good (that is, of the moral order in human life and in nature); (c) the omnipotence of the divine will can guarantee a completion of all aspects of the human good, internal and external; (d) granted that His relationship to us is truly inter-personal, final human good can plausibly be seen as living a life in perfected relationship with Him.

If we think of divine will as order-creating then a theistic foundation for ethics can be seen as giving ethics an aretaic structure. The right will not be primarily that which is expressly commanded by God. It will be that which embodies respect for the good that the divine order lays down as the best way in which a human life is to be lived. Theistic ethics is a distinctive form of aretaic theory in at least two respects. First it offers its own account of how the human good is possible and capable of attainment. Second it provides its own distinctive vision of what that good consists in, a vision which flows from a specific account of human nature and circumstances. There is no reason, however, to expect anything other than large overlaps between a theistically inspired aretaic theory and a secular one. For one thing, the theistic account will inevitably bring with it a distinction between the relationship between divine will and human ethics in the order of knowing and in the order of being. In the order of knowing it seems right to say that most will know of divine will through knowing what are and what are not choiceworthy human acts, what is and is not mandated by reason in conduct. The divine will cannot create a moral order in the world which human beings participate in unless they are able to discern the demands of moral reason for themselves (compare Meynell 1972:228–29). In the order of knowing the operations of conscience will come first even though in the order of creation it is divine will that has shaped the facts and circumstances on which human reason gets to work. Because of this distinction between orders of knowing and being, it should be expected that ethical knowledge is widely available and not confined to those who have explicit faith in God. Only an insistence on a very radical account of human falleness could provide an escape from this conclusion. But such an account, if it told us that there was no ordinary, reliable human perception of the good would land us back in the paradoxes of the first horn of the Euthyphro dilemma.

Having got thus far, we can return to the defining features of morality. A modified divine command theory of the type outlined appears to have no problem in explaining how morality can be rational, authoritative and universal. Rationality can be secured because there is a moral background to acceptance of the express commands of God. Moreover, many ordinary moral requirements are perceived to exist simply through the operation of reason upon human nature and circumstances. The authority of moral principles is likewise explained through their being backed by reasons relating to the ultimate human good. Morality can be expected to be universal if the divine will creates a moral order in which we all share by virtue of being creatures possessed of human aptitudes and reason. The distinction between orders of knowing and being enshrines the thought that we should know of the requirements of morality independently of knowing their ontological foundation. So that those ignorant, from the theistic point of view, of the true foundations of morality are nonetheless capable of reasoning and acting like moral beings. If it is the fact that they are created (and thus members of moral order) that makes them moral beings, rather than that they are card-carrying members of a particular faith or denomination, then we should expect all human beings to be sharers of moral knowledge.

For the reasons outlined above we can expect the theistic outlook to preserve the autonomy of the moral agent. Normal moral judgements will properly be the outcome of conscientious and rational thought on the part of moral agents. Even express divine commands will be accepted because of a perception of the morally-rich property of authority in the source of those commands. In the Judaic and Christian traditions episodes of divine commanding are more properly seen as events in a continuing relationship of covenant between God and His people and it is essential to the good achievable in this relationship that the human side to it preserves its autonomy. The aim of the relationship is after all to enable the human side to it to grow in love and fellowship with the Lord, not to be reduced to His automata.

What besets writers such as Nowell-Smith and Rachels who are critical of theistic theories of ethics is the 'Abraham and Isaac syndrome'. If God did *per impossible* command something we perceived to be wicked, would we not have to abandon our autonomy and do it nonetheless? Even to be ready in principle to do seems incompatible with one's role as an autonomous moral agent. However, if we give the will of God the right moral and epistemological background much of the sting of this puzzle is removed. With that background express commands of God will be reliable pointers, to say the least, to the rightness of acts. So what we are faced with is the problem of a conflict in two putatively trustworthy indicators of what is right: our judgement based on moral factors minus what is allegedly revealed about God's commandments and our judgement about the direction of divine will. True judgement based on these two different grounds will be in harmony, since God is good. Conflict will create the the problem of which set of factors has been rightly interpreted. In resolving this problem the believer remains an autonomous agent if he or she exercises freedom of mind and will in deciding which factors are to be trusted in judging what is to be done, and if that judgement is then honoured in action. But the necessity to preserve these forms of moral integrity do not explain why a putative divine prescription should not be the crucial factor in deciding whether some act is right (Coulter 1989:121).

Appeal to autonomy can only decisively rule out a grounding of moral values and moral knowledge in divine will if it has a richer sense than personal integrity in making and acting on choices.

Following Kant, some authors wish to interpret the autonomy of moral agents as the ability, indeed necessity, of each of us to choose or legislate our own moral principles. We have met already in a number of contexts the idea that morality is not discovered but invented or chosen. The existence of an authoritative source of moral judgement independent of human agents would be a threat to this kind of autonomy. But it is not clear whether this type of autonomy is at all valuable. On the surface it is incompatible not merely with theistic ethics but with any view that regards moral judgement as answerable to reasons independent of human preferences and choices. On any view of morality as discovered, conscientious judgements may always be open to criticism on external grounds and face the possibility of having to defer to external sources of guidance. (For a full discussion of the modern notion of autonomy and divine commands see Coulter 1989.)

We have followed an essentially Thomistic solution to the philosophical problems in linking morality to a theistic outlook. This links morality and the will of God without making the former arbitrary and non-universal by stressing the character of the divine-human relationship as a moral one and by pointing to the way in which the divine will creates a moral order which is open to human judgement. One final question needs to be considered about this scheme. It relates to the *extent* to which moral value arises out of the divine creative will. This question can be asked first about the extent to which human ethics so arises and second about the extent to which value in general so arises.

Consider the range of rules and principles that form human ethics. Many of them look as if they are necessarily true, if true at all. Examine the moral principles that grow out of the conventions that are necessary for moral relationships such as friendship. We have argued (Chapter 2) that such principles are true because constitutive of the very nature of such relationships. They do not represent contingent facts whose character depends therefore on the direction of the creator's will. At most we might say that God is responsible for a universe in which it is possible for the relationship of friendship to be exemplified, but not for the truth of the moral principles that grow out of the very nature of the relationship (compare Helm 1981:9–10). It looks as if there is a range of moral principles which are necessarily true and which depend on God's will (in the same manner as the principles of arithmetic) not for their truth but for their exemplification in this world (Swinburne 1981 argues this case).

There is no reason to deny the general point that moral knowledge is a mixture, like other forms of human cognition, of necessary and contingent truths. It appears to be a contingent fact, though a deeply embedded one, that the world in which we live makes courage a moral virtue. It is contingently true that the world we live in faces us with temptations, dangers and trials, and that human choices are made or marred by the way in which we face up to these. It appears to be a non-contingent fact, arising out of the conventions which define the nature of the act, that making a promise creates a *prima facie* obligation to fulfill it. Now it is a theological orthodoxy, reflecting the way in which we must think of necessary truth, that divine power cannot extend to the making and unmaking of necessary truth. Thus it cannot extend to the making and unmaking of any moral principles that are necessary (for a dissenting view see Devine 1989:89–90). But before we conclude that this limits severely the extent to which God may be the source of morality, we should remind ourselves that on the aretaic conception of ethics ethical judgement focuses around the uniting conception of the good: the best, most worthwhile and praiseworthy life for a human being. Only thus unified can it expect to have a proper account of moral motivation and of the ranking of moral principles. Contingent and necessary moral truths must be somehow incorporated into such a conception. It is not difficult to see how this may be done. Recognition of the necessarily true moral principles that arise out of the structure of human, moral relationships is a component part of the good because we have a social nature which flourishes through the sharing of interests with others that such relationships make possible. It could have been otherwise. Creatures less social by nature would not have found their flourishing promoted by acquiring the extended personal interests that tend to fuse their private goods with the goods of others. It looks as if the final place of any moral principles in promotion of the good depends on their being an economy in human nature which is contingent in the last analysis. A creator God would be the ultimate source of all morality in the sense that His will was the ground of the nature and possibility of final good for human beings. He is the source of this economy in human nature and of the fact, if it is a fact, that reality is such as to finally satisfy it.

We may say on the aretaic view that God's will is the ultimate source of human goodness and that such goodness is independent of human choice and decision. But it seems that at a deeper level this view must leave some value independent of God and his creative will. To avoid the paradoxes of the Euthyphro dilemma we have had to say that there are some values and requirements which are not created by the divine will and to which it must conform if it is in turn to create values. The relationship between God and His human creatures must be morally structured if it is to be the source of new obligations. God must minimally be good if is will is to create a genuine moral order. If we say that God's being good merely consists in Him being consistent with His own will (because the divine will creates all goodness after all) we are back with the paradoxes of Euthyphro. 'God is good' would be a miserable tautology and arbitrariness would have been reintroduced into ethics once more. To avoid this it looks as though we must conclude that, for the divine will to serve as the ground of further values, it must itself be subject to some independent principles of value. It is good and capable of creating a moral order only if it is so subject. Hence some value (perhaps represented by uncreated necessarily true principles) is metaphysically independent of God.

For the reasons outlined in this chapter this metaphysical claim does not disturb the point that moral value for *human creatures* may be derived from their relation to God. But the limitation on divine creativity remains a problem for metaphysics and philosophy of religion. One solution to it is worth mentioning. William Alston (1989:253–73) suggests that we distinguish between the divine nature and the divine will. The divine will is good and value creating because in the last analysis it conforms to what is good independently of it. However, it may be that the paradigm of metaphysically ultimate value to which it conforms is the divine nature, thought of as something separate from divine decrees and commands. The final exemplar of value is not the divine will but God's nature, viewed as analogous in this respect to the form of the good in Plato's philosophy. Things have value in so far as they resemble or participate in this nature. The key metaphysical claim about goodness that theism makes on this view is that our standard of goodness is not an ideal entity or abstract principle (such as Plato's Form is) but a concrete being which is also the creative source of reality.

CONVERGENCE AND DIVERGENCE IN ETHICS

In the preceding section I have argued for the possibility of a religious basis to ethics. I have re-deployed an aretaic conception of ethics in doing so. One of the advantages of the structure of aretaic theorising in ethics is that it allows for what seems obvious to reflection: that there can be both convergence and dialogue between secular and religious ethics, on the one hand, and yet also divergence and disagreement, on the other.

Convergence is implied through the fact that some moral judgement is not affected by disagreements over the shape of the final good for humanity. Not all moral reasoning depends on arguing down from a worked out conception of the good; some springs from immediacies of moral circumstance that will be evident to a wide range of outlooks on the good. Moreover, it is of the essence of the aretaic view that the test of a moral claim is the sense it makes of human experiences of choice and decision. Agreement is also implied because there will be points of overlap between conceptions of the good. So though there will be differences in the accounts of the virtues offered by religious and secular ethical systems, there will be many points of contact at the level of reflection on the virtues and at stages of moral reasoning below this level.

Divergence is implied because at key points secular and religious thinkers will offer different accounts of human nature, the reality that surrounds it and thus of its destiny. There will also be divergence because different outlooks will tend to give different descriptions of human action. To take a simple case: if someone without faith gives a cheque to disaster relief he or she can be described as helping fellow human beings in need and as exhibiting solidarity with human suffering. If one who has a Christian faith does likewise, he or she could describe the act as, in addition, serving God and witnessing to common fellowship in Christ. Aquinas' example, discussed in Chapter 3, of the act of theft that acquires the new character of sacrilege illustrates the extent to which the moral universe may have different character for those with different outlooks upon it (for further discussion of this point see Sutherland 1982).

Secular and religious outlooks will each give their own interpetation of each other. To the secularist, a Christian or other religously influenced ethical outlook will rest on a partly insightful, partly mistaken vision of the world. To the religious outlook, secular ethics will share to some extent in the knowledge of God's will in creation and divine grace in the making of moral judgements. There is no reason why secular moral judgement should not be regarded as enshrining genuine experience of the good. But it will lack the final means of integrating its insights that comes from an acknowledgment of the divine scheme in creation and will be deficient in the hope that comes from that acknowledgement (compare Mahoney 1987 chapter eight).

On an aretaic view there is every reason to expect dialogue between different ethical outlooks with different accounts of the human good, especially as it stresses the worth of first-hand experience in the making of choices as a source of moral insight. However this is not good enough for some. From some religious thinkers comes the claim that since secular ethics lacks, on their view, the final truth about the good, so none of its insights are worthwhile. From some secular thinkers comes the claim that the essence of morality leaves no room for worthwhile religious reasoning to moral conclusions.

The first of these criticisms of dialogue and consensus between secular and religious ethics is illustrated in Oliver O'Donovan's statement that ' . . . knowledge of the moral order is a grasp of the total shape in which, if anything is lacking, everthing is lacking' (1986:89). We have already conceded the the point that, from the religious point of view, something must be lacking in the secular conception of the moral order. Whether O'Donovan's implication follows depends once more on the moral epistemology one brings to ethical theory. Here I can only stress again the 'bottom-up' nature of much moral reasoning according to the aretaic conception favoured in this study. On this view knowledge of fundamental moral principle and full insight into the virtues is a function of moral goodness and the experience which lies behind acquiring that. It follows that moral judgement is at all times and for all individuals (regardless of whether they have been granted the right metaphysical beliefs or not) growing to maturity and reliablity. Maturity in judgment is a process rather than an achievement for all. This I suggest would destroy the basis of O'Donovan's implicit contrast between those outlooks which have the complete picture and those which do not.

The second criticism builds upon the idea discussed in earlier chapters that the form of morality restricts the extent to which any religious principles can properly influence ethics. To take stock of this idea properly we must return to arguments already aired in the discussion of utilitarianism in Chapter 3. What is important here is the idea of universality. Unlike the values established by appetite moral values should be recognizable by and commendable to all. This is a thought that we have supported throughout this study. But claims about the character of moral value can be commended to all only if three conditions are met: they must be supported by impersonal reasons, they must not depend directly upon personal feelings, and any facts offered in their favour must be subject to empirical confirmation (Sumner 1981:37–38). This last condition has been held to be necessarily violated by any religious metaphysic behind a moral outlook:

> Since science is our established procedure for confirming or disconfirming beliefs about the world, factual claims must be subject to some form of empirical verification. This condition entails that, unless some form of natural theology is correct, religious beliefs cannot count as reasons in favour of a moral view . . . If a natural theology *is* correct, then religion is a part of science and its claims are empirically testable. Otherwise those claims are supernatural, beyond confirmation or disconfirmation. Such claims cannot be impersonal reasons. (Sumner 1981:38)

Granted this conception of the nature of reason in ethics, then the influence of faith upon morality can be no more than that of the influence of personal and private feelings. Dialogue between different moral outlooks is possible and worthwhile provided that the reasons they offer for moral judgements are translatable into a common language of scientifically testable opinion. The effect of this qualification on worthwhile dialogue is thus to exclude religious ethics from taking part by dismissing its claim to have a valid *moral* (that is universal, impersonal) outlook. Thus Sumner, from whom we have quoted, wishes to mediate between opposing views on the ethics of abortion without having to take into account various Christian views on the nature of human life – on the ground that these can only be based on personal faith, not scientific reason. The form the mediation takes is, naturally, the translation of different views into a utilitarian idiom.

Here we see confirmation of the importance of contemporary moral theory for thought about the foundations of moral theology. The desire for 'scientific ethics' gets its concrete exemplification in those philosophical theories of morality which hope to construct a decision procedure for ethics. We have noted in the case of contemporary consequentialist and deontological thought the goal of producing a method for ethics using procedural rules derived from the essence of morality or reason applied to research into states of pleasure and pain or into the state of people's preferences. Only if such a method can be found and made to work does the secular critic of religious ethics have a real, not notional or wishful, contrast between 'scientific' secular ethics and 'personal' religious outlook.

One of the major themes of this book has been to argue against the contrast that Sumner and others offer us. In Chapter 2 I endeavoured to show how there could be genuine forms of argument which did not follow standard pictures of inductive and deductive reasoning. In discussion of philosophical moral theories I tried to indicate that philosophy cannot produce a decision procedure for ethics. I have criticised the idea that a simple conception of the good plus some procedural rules derived from the essence of rationality or morals will be enough to deduce a worthwhile system of ethics. I have asserted the relevance of large-scale conceptions of the nature of humanity and reality to the determination of the virtues and the forms of human good. I have implied that contemporary consequentialist and deontological theorising are in reality pictures – not without their own insights and merits – into the nature of the human good which must be defended like others.

So if the fundamental argument of this book is sound Sumner's reasons for rejecting dialogue with religious ethics are mistaken because based on untenable contrasts. There are however more subtle challenges behind his arguments. If our fundamental thought about the universality of ethics is correct, then any outlook on human nature and the world that claims to possess moral insight must consider how that insight can be publicly commended and shared. If it cannot be, then its claim to be insight is open to question. It must be truth backed by publicly defensible reason. But any form of religious ethics will want to avoid the conclusion that the way in which moral insight can become publicly commendable is through its translation into an idiom which can stand as the lowest common denominator of public debate. For that idiom will be one in which the possibility of a Christian or Jewish or any kind of religious ethics is lost.

The argument points to one extreme to be avoided: purchasing the universality of ethics at the cost of reducing its resources to a set of concepts and judgements neutral as between all outlooks. Any specific moral outlook can rightly object that this would be unfair to its claim to have the true account of the human good. Moreover from a general point of view it is likely to lead to the impoverishment of moral thought, since it will close up sources of insight and reflection. We might then fly to the opposite extreme and say that the demand for universality is misleading. Since Christian ethics, for example, claims to have moral insight based upon truth, it can be publicly shared but only at the cost of first persuading all of the full truth of the Christian outlook. This in effect ends dialogue and negates the idea that moral experience might be an area in which shared experience of value was possible and swapping of insights from different outlooks desirable.

Somehow there must be a way of mediating between these two extremes on dialogue in ethics. This would be a way of holding in creative tension two thoughts, both of which have been supported in this study. On the one hand we naturally think of there being something that is morality: the precise content of which 'we' debate and in which 'our' minds meet. On the other hand we naturally think of their being distinct perspectives in this shared something: Christian, Jewish, humanist, Islamic and so on. I offer two final reflections on this paradox.

It may be that the paradox is not peculiar to ethics and is an instance of a more a general tension between universal and particular in knowledge which we normally think can be overcome. For each of us is a unique centre of consciousness and experience. Each of us embodies a unique point of view upon the world. Yet the thing we call 'human knowledge' is possible only because the experiences gained from these unique vantage points are shareable and shared. That is one way we distinguish knowledge from illusion. The enlargement of human knowledge is only possible because we recognise both that there are distinct vantage points upon reality, so insight comes from all quarters, and that there are ways in which these distinct vantages contribute to a whole.

One of the fundamental insights of the Aristotelian tradition is that ethics is a practical science. Its aim is not right belief but right action. Excellence in it is excellence in the making of choices not in the devising or discovery of theories or metaphysical systems. The insight that matters in it is the insight that is proved in the making of choices. This has been a familiar theme in this study. It suggests a way in which divergent starting points in ethics can be accepted, without desire to reduce them to a lowest common denominator of outlook. They can be accepted because they lead to insight at the point where it matters.

If there is a form of the experience of value rooted at the level of making decisions as to which acts are choiceworthy and which not, then there is a way of testing, using and sharing the moral knowledge that each distinct outlook on human nature and circumstances claims to offer.

Works Cited

Alston W. 1989, 'Some suggestions for divine command theorists' in W. Alston *Divine Nature and Human Language* (Ithaca: Cornell University Press), 253–273.

Aquinas, 1966a, *Summa Theologiae* vol. 18, 1a 2ae 18–21, tr T. Gilby (London: Blackfriars).

——, 1966b, *Summa Theologiae* vol. 28, 1a 2ae 90–97, tr T. Gilby (London: Blackfriars).

Aristotle, 1925a, *Nicomachean Ethics* tr W. D. Ross in *The Works of Aristotle Translated into English*, vol. 9 (Oxford: Clarendon Press).

——, 1925b, *Eudemian Ethics* tr J. Solomon in *The Works of Aristotle Translated into English*, vol. 9 (Oxford: Clarendon Press).

Bambrough, R. 1979, *Moral Scepticism and Moral Knowledge* (London: Routledge).

Bond, E. J., 1988, *Reason and Value* (Cambridge: Cambridge University Press).

Braithwaite, R. B., 1966, 'An empiricist's account of the nature of religious belief', in I. T. Ramsey (ed.), *Christian Ethics and Contemporary Philosophy* (London: SCM,) 53–73.

Bratman, M., 1987, *Intentions, Plans and Practical Reason* (Cambridge Mass.: Harvard University Press).

Brennan, J. M., 1977, *The Open Texture of Moral Concepts* (London: Macmillan).

Brown, A., 1986, *Modern Political Philosophy* (Harmondsworth: Penguin).

Byrne, P., 1979, 'Leavis, literary criticism and philosophy' in *British Journal of Aesthetics*, vol. 19, no. 3, 263–273.

——, 1990, 'Homicide, medical ethics and the principle of double effect' in P. Byrne (ed.), *Ethics and Law in Health Care and Research* (Chichester: Wiley) 131–160.

Coulter, C. L., 1989, 'Moral autonomy and divine commands' in *Religious Studies*, vol. 25 no. 1, 117–129.

Crombie, 1966, 'Moral Principles' in I. T. Ramsey (ed.), *Christian Ethics and Contemporary Philosophy* (London: SCM) 234–261.

Cupitt, D., 1980, *Taking Leave of God* (London: SCM).

D'Arcy, E., 1963 *Human Acts* (Oxford: Clarendon Press).

Dent, N. J. H., 1984, *The Moral Psychology of the Virtues* (Cambridge: Cambridge University Press).

Devine, P., 1978 *The Ethics of Homicide* (Ithaca: Cornell University Press).

——, 1989, *Relativism, Nihilism and God* (Notre Dame, Indiania: University of Notre Dame Press).

Dickens, C., 1969, *Hard Times* (Harmondsworth: Penguin).

Edgely, R., 1969, *Reason in Theory and Practice* (London: Hutchinson).

Fairweather, I. C. M., and MacDonald, J. I. H., 1984, *The Quest for Christian Ethics* (Edinburgh: Handsel Press).

Finnis, J., 1980, *Natural Law and Natural Rights* (Oxford: Clarendon Press).

——, 1983, *The Fundamentals of Ethics* (Oxford: Oxford University Press).

Frankena, W., 1981, 'Is morality logically dependent on religion?' in P. Helm (ed.), *Divine Commands and Morality* (Oxford: Oxford University Press) 14–33.

Frey, R. G., 1984a, 'Introduction: utilitarianism and persons' in R. G. Frey (ed.), *Utility and Rights* (Oxford: Blackwell), 3–19.

——, 1984b, 'Act-utilitarianism, consequentialism, and moral rights' in R. G. Frey (ed.), *Utility and Rights* (Oxford: Blackwell) 61–85.

Gauthier, D., 1986, *Morals by Agreement* (Oxford: Clarendon Press).

Geach, P., 1969, *God and the Soul* (London: Routledge).

Gert, B., 1973, *The Moral Rules* (New York: Harper & Row).

Green, R., 1978, *Religious Reason* (New York: Oxford University Press).

Griffin, J., 1986, *Well-Being* (Oxford: Clarendon Press).

Hampshire, S., 1977, *Two Theories of Morality* (Oxford: British Academy/Oxford University Press).

Hare, R. M., 1963, *Freedom and Reason* (Oxford: Clarendon Press).

——, 1981, *Moral Thinking* (Oxford: Clarendon Press).

Harrison, B., 1984 'Moral judgement, action and emotion' in *Philosophy*, vol. 59, no. 229, 295–322.

——, 1989, 'Morality and interest' in *Philosophy*, vol. 64, no. 249, 303–322.

Helm, P., 1981, 'Introduction' in P. Helm (ed.), *Divine Commands and Morality* (Oxford: Oxford University Press) 1–13.

Hutchinson, D. S., 1986, *The Virtues of Aristotle* (London: Routledge).

Kant I., 1956, *Critique of Practical Reason* tr L. W. Beck (Indianapolis: Bobbs Merill).

——, 1959, *Foundations of the Metaphysics of Morals* tr L. W. Beck (Indianapolis: Bobbs-Merill).

——, 1965, *The Metaphysical Elements of Justice* tr J. Ladd (Indianapolis: Bobbs-Merill).

——, 1971, *The Doctrine of Virtue* tr M. J. Gregor (Philadelphia: University of Pennsylvania Press).

Kekes, J., 1990, *Facing Evil* (Princeton: Princeton University Press).

Kirk, K., 1933, *Conscience and its Problems* (London: Longmans).

Locke, J., 1975, *An Essay Concerning Human Understanding* (Oxford: Clarendon Press).

——, 1978, *A Letter Concerning Toleration* (Indianapolis: Bobbs-Merril).

Lucas, J., 1980, *On Justice* (Oxford: Clarendon Press).

MacIntyre, A., 1967, *Secularisation and Moral Change* (Oxford: Oxford University Press).

Mackie, J. L., 1977, *Ethics: Inventing Right and Wrong* (Harmondsworth: Penguin).

MacNaughton, D., 1988, *Moral Vision* (Oxford: Blackwell).

Mahoney, J., 1987, *The Making of Moral Theology* (Oxford: Clarendon Press).

Meynell H., 1972, 'The Euthyphro dilemma' in *Aristotelian Society Supplementary Volume*, 223–234.

Mitchell, B. G., 1980, *Morality: Religious and Secular* (Oxford: Clarendon Press).

Munro, 1967, *Empiricism and Ethics* (Cambridge: Cambridge University Press).

Nagel, T., 1978, *The Possibility of Altruism* (Princeton: Princeton University Press).

Nowell, Smith, P. H., 1954, *Ethics* (Harmondsworth: Penguin).

——, 1966, 'Morality: religious and secular' in I. T. Ramsey (ed.), *Christian Ethics and Contemporary Philosophy* (London: SCM) 95–112.

O'Donovan, O., 1986, *Resurrection and the Moral Order* (London: Inter Varsity Press).

O'Neill, O., 1980, 'The most extensive liberty' in *Proceedings of the Aristotelian Society 1979–80*, vol. 80, 45–60.

Plato, 1963, *Euthyphro* in E. Hamilton and H. Cairns (eds), *The Complete Dialogues* (Princeton NJ: Princeton University Press), 169–185.

Rachels, J., 1981, 'God and human attitudes' in P. Helm (ed.), *Divine Commands and Morality* (Oxford: Oxford University Press) 34–48.

Rawls J., 1972, *A Theory of Justice* (Oxford: Oxford University Press).

Raz J., 1984, 'Rights-based moralities' in R. G. Frey (ed.), *Utility and Rights* (Oxford: Blackwell) 42–60.

Sandel, M. J., 1982, *Liberalism and the Limits of Justice* (Cambridge: Cambridge University Press).

Scruton, R., 1986, *Sexual Desire* (London: Weidenfeld & Nicholson).

Sherman, N., 1989, *The Fabric of Character* (Oxford: Clarendon Press).

Smart, J. J. C., 1973, 'An outline of a system of utilitarian ethics' in J. J. C. Smart and B. Williams *Utilitarianism: For and Against* (Cambridge: Cambridge University Press) 3–74.

Sumner, L. W., 1981, *Abortion and Moral Theory* (Princeton: Princeton University Press).

——, 1987, *The Moral Foundation of Rights* (Oxford: Clarendon Press).

Sutherland, S. R., 1982, 'Religion, ethics and action' in S. R. Sutherland and B. Hebblethwaite (eds), *The Philosophical Frontiers of Christian Theology* (Cambridge: Cambridge University Press) 153–167.

Swinburne, R. G., 1981, 'Duty and the will of God' in P. Helm (ed.), *Divine Commands and Morality* (Oxford: Oxford University Press) 120–134.

Thompson, J. J., 1986, 'A defence of abortion' in W. Parent (ed.), *Rights, Restitution and Risk* (Cambridge Mass.: Harvard University Press) 1–19.

van den Beld, 1988, 'Killing and the principle of double effect' in *Scottish Journal of Theology*, vol. 41, no. 1, 93–116.

Warnock, G. J., 1967, *Contemporary Moral Philosophy* (London: Macmillan).

Wertheimer, R., 1972, *The Significance of Sense* (Ithaca: Cornell University Press).

White, A. R., 1970, *Truth* (London: Macmillan).

Wiggins, D., 1991, 'Moral cognition, moral relativism and motivating moral beliefs' in *Proceedings of the Aristotelian Society, 1990–91* vol. 91, 161–86.

Williams, B., 1972, *Morality* (Harmondsworth: Penguin).

——, 1985, *Ethics and the Limits of Philosophy* (London: Collins).

Wisdom, J., 1965, *Paradox and Discovery* (Oxford: Blackwell).

Wittgenstein, L., 1953, *Philosophical Investigations* (Oxford: Blackwell).

Index